THE TRUTH ABOUT
TRUST
IN BUSINESS

How to Enrich the Bottom Line, Improve Retention,
and Build Valuable Relationships for Success

D1518216

VANESSA HALL

WITH CONTRIBUTIONS BY MANDY HOLLOWAY, JAMES ADONIS,
FIONA PEARMAN, DAVID PENGLASE, AND IVEN FRANGI

EMERALD
BOOK CO.
A Division of Greenleaf Book Group LLC

Published by Emerald Book Company
Austin, TX
www.emeraldbookcompany.com

Distributed by Emerald Book Company

For ordering information or special discounts for bulk purchases, please contact Emerald Book Company at PO Box 91869, Austin, TX 78709, 512.891.6100.

Design and composition by Greenleaf Book Group LLC
Cover design by Greenleaf Book Group LLC

The term ENP is a trademark registered with IP Australia and the Australian Government and is owned by the author's company, Entente Pty Limited.

Cataloging-in-Publication data

ISBN 13: TK

Part of the Tree Neutral™ program, which offsets the number of trees consumed in the production and printing of this book by taking proactive steps, such as planting trees in direct proportion to the number of trees used: www. treeneutral.com
[COMP: Insert TN logo to right of above blurb]

TreeNeutral

Printed in the United States of America on acid-free paper

09 10 11 12 13 14 10 9 8 7 6 5 4 3 2 1

First Edition

CONTENTS

So essentially vital is the commodity of trust; the glue in every interaction that we have. And so few have explored it so insightfully and comprehensively as Vanessa Hall has. A mind-stretching and life-changing read.

—ALLAN PARKER, INTERNATIONAL NEGOTIATOR, EDUCATOR, AND BEST-SELLING AUTHOR OF *Switch on Your Brain* AND *The Negotiator's Toolkit*

INTRODUCTION

WHY A BOOK ABOUT TRUST?

Trust. It's one of those words we use all the time. We hear it on the radio and TV. We all know that when trust is broken it can be one of the most painful experiences of our lives. So why write a book about something we already know about?

Well, first, I challenge the notion that we actually know about trust. From my experience it is one of those things we think we know but it is usually a surface knowledge. Second, it is so critical to building relationships, both professionally and personally (and that is one thing that everyone seems to agree on), that I think it warrants exploring and understanding.

WHAT MAKES THIS BOOK DIFFERENT?

Now, this is not the first time someone has written about trust. In fact, philosophers have studied it, academics have lectured on it, and some great books have been written about it. What makes this book different? A few key things:

1. I have developed a series of models and diagrams that actually describe what trust is. Th ese have been shown to everyone from kids to CEOs to psychologists to college professors. Everyone loves them—now it's your turn to see them!

2. This book takes a practical approach to exploring trust and teaching companies what they need to do to build and maintain it across various aspects of business. It is filled with tips and guidance and real case studies to show you that it does really work.

3. I have included in this book the collective wisdom of known leaders in their fields. They, more than anyone, can give you all the guidance you need to make a real difference in your organization.

4. This book gives you insights and understanding in an easy-to-read style. Personally, I hate to read textbooks. I like to understand the author of the book—to know what makes her or him tick—because it deepens the message that individual is delivering. I hope when you reach the end of this book you will feel like you know me, and the other authors as well.

WHY ME?

Interestingly, I have been asking myself this question for the eighteen months I have been contemplating and planning this book!

Let me say, outright, that I am not an academic. I am not a psychologist. I am a thirty-nine-year-old woman who has had this concept of trust buzzing around in my head for so long that I finally thought, "I have to write a book." The messages here can and have helped people—lots of people.

Let me tell you some of the reasons why the whole concept of trust and these models are so important to me.

First, my son, Lachlan, who was nine at the time, brought home a one-page description of "My Mum" that he had made at school for Mother's

Day. Here is a copy of it; see if you can spot the thing that jumped out at me!

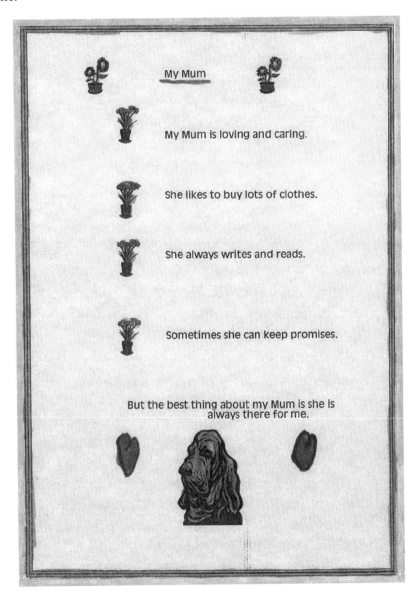

Immediately after the "Awww, that's lovely. Thank you," I then said, "What do you mean I *sometimes* keep promises?" I was quite indignant. "That's not me!" I thought.

"Well, sometimes you don't keep your promises," Lachlan said, very matter of fact.

"Can you give me an example?" I asked. I was a bit confused at this point.

"Like the other week, you said we might go and see a movie on the weekend, and then we didn't go," he replied with a pout.

"Oh, that's OK. It wasn't really a promise, then, right?"

Lachlan looked at me and said, "*I* thought it was."

Reflecting on what I had said, I then realize that, whether I meant it as a promise or not, that was how my son had perceived it.

I started thinking about all the times I say things like that, not only to him but also at work and to friends. My head started spinning. I pulled myself together and asked, "How did that make you feel?" I reached out and touched his hand.

He looked me squarely in the eyes and said, "I just don't know when I can trust you." I felt like someone had reached in and ripped my heart out.

My son taught me a great lesson that day, and it was the start of the development of the model we will explore throughout this book.

Second, I have worked in compliance and risk management for most of my career, predominantly in financial services in Australia. What I have seen over the years is an industry that has had some difficulty in regulating itself, together with a string of corporate collapses, fraud, and questionable deals that has eroded trust in a vital industry.

Let me tell you, these companies are not all bad. In fact, I have always believed that, fundamentally, most people actually want to do the right thing. More often than not, many of them just don't know what the right thing is, or the laws have become so complex and open to interpretation it has become increasingly difficult to know what is right by law and what is right ethically—and often the two don't match.

Interestingly, humans often have a habit of generalizing, and recently the professionals in the financial services industry have born the brunt of such sweeping criticisms as "all financial planners are unethical," or "all stockbrokers are greedy." Other industries have suffered the same for a long time: for example, "all real estate agents are self-serving," and so on. What happens when generalizations like this are spoken is that trust breaks down, and everyone is tarred with the same brush. From a purely compliance perspective, that means everyone must meet more stringent regulations. This will be explored more in part 3.

Basically, my experience in this particular field tells me that a breakdown of trust causes a lot of pain and expense for business, most of which can be avoided.

As I became interested in the whole concept of trust concept and began working on ways to describe what I believed, I also began talking to lots of people. I met with and ran workshops with CEOs, small business owners, marketing and branding staff, sales managers, HR managers, customer service representatives, compliance professionals, regulators, fraud investigators, police, consultants, and general employees. What I found was this:

1. 99 percent of those interviewed agreed that trust was a critical component of a strong relationship.
2. About 90 percent had some difficulty describing just exactly what trust is.
3. 99 percent said that when trust was broken, it either could not be repaired or it would take a very long time to restore it.
4. 95 percent said they did not consciously and actively build trust in their organizations.

Need I say more?

WHAT CAN YOU EXPECT FROM READING THIS BOOK?

As you will see, one of the core components of building trust is to manage expectations. So, I thought I should walk the talk (also a quality of a trustworthy person) by listing what you can expect from reading my book.

1. A greater awareness of the importance of trust in business
2. An understanding of what trust actually is

3. Knowledge of how to build trust
4. Knowledge of how to ensure that trust, once you have established it, is not broken
5. Practical guidance on how to become more trustworthy
6. Practical advice about how to build trustworthy brands and businesses
7. Insights from leaders in their fields of business
8. Information on how to find people to support you in building trust in your business

At the end of each chapter I have added a feature called "Something to Do" to help you deepen your knowledge and experience of understanding and building trust.

I hope you enjoy reading this book and that you will continue to use it as a guide. My wish for you is that you are able to build and maintain trust in your business and reap the rewards personally and professionally.

Vanessa Hall

Winter 2009

PART 1

TRUST 101:
A REVIEW OF THE BASICS

1

LET'S DEFINE TRUST

*Just as trust is the key to all relationships, so also is trust
the glue of organization. It is the cement that holds the bricks together.*
—Stephen Covey, The 8th Habit: From Effectiveness to Greatness

When I run workshops on trust, one of the first things I do is ask people to do a little exercise to get them thinking about trust. You can do this too.

First, close your eyes and think about the person in your life you trust the most. What words come to mind when you think of that individual?

Here are the top five responses I've tallied from workshop participants:

1. Honest
2. Genuine
3. Has integrity
4. Displays selflessness
5. Does what they say they will do

Now, think about the person in your life you trust the least. What words come to mind when you think of that individual?

Here are the top five responses I've tallied from workshop participants (the ones we could print, anyway!):

1. Dishonest
2. Selfish
3. Scheming
4. Incongruent
5. Backstabbing

Now, think about what it would take for you to trust such a person again.

In my experience, there have only ever been two responses:

1. I would never trust that person again. (99 percent)
2. It would take a long time before I would trust him/her again, and I'd probably still have doubts. (1 percent)

What this tells me about trust in business is that you had better be pretty careful not to completely lose the trust of your staff, management, customers, partners, shareholders, or board of directors, because if you do, the chances of you getting it back again are miniscule.

Although we may choose to forgive a person or a company, we may still never fully trust them again. You'll see what I mean as you read on.

SO, WHAT IS TRUST?

The *Oxford English Dictionary* defines trust as:

- A firm belief in the reliability, truth, ability or strength of someone or something
- Confident expectation
- To place trust in, believe in, rely on the character or behavior of
- To have faith, confidence or hope that a thing will take place

In 2006, my company, Entente Pty Limited, commissioned Taverner Research to interview six hundred people across Australia and asked them this simple question: What is trust? Here are some of the varied responses we received:

> Knowing that you can depend on somebody so that they would do what they say they would do and they are reliable.
>
> It is just being honest with somebody; you feel safe with them and [believe that] what they say is honest.
>
> I suppose having absolute confidence in a person to keep me safe and to keep any confidence that I might have in them. It would be a two-way thing. They would have trust in me.
>
> It's a cornerstone of human civilization. It's your bond between one human being and another. It's a value.
>
> It means you can depend on someone.
>
> Trust is a close correlation between what an individual says and what they actually do. I would trust someone if what they say and what they do actually matches up.
>
> Having confidence in the situation or the person you are dealing with that you won't be deceived or misled.

I discovered that the word for trust in Spanish is "confianza," and in French, "confiance" is the word for the "feeling of trust" or "reliance." So, this concept of being able to rely on or have confidence in something is intimately connected with the word "trust."

I've spent a lot of time talking to many people about what trust means to them, and this is how I now define "trust":

> The ability to rely on a
>> Person
>> Company
>> Product or Service
> to deliver an outcome.

For clarity, when I talk about a "person," this could also include a spiritual being—as in the expression, "I trust in God"—or an animal. (I thought I'd better include that because one day someone is going to say, "But what about my dog? I trust my dog!" So, dogs are included.)

When I talk about a "company," this is the interaction you, as a customer or an employee, might have with a company. We might say we trust a particular company, like Colgate or Cadburys—both of which, incidentally, are often identified as trustworthy companies in opinion polls and surveys.

When I talk about a product or service, this is intended to capture most everything, from a pen to a car to a telecommunications service.

But what is this outcome we are relying on someone or something to deliver? It is different for every person, and different in every situation. We could be relying on a company to keep paying us every two weeks, relying on a café to deliver a hot, steaming mug of coffee, or relying on our car to start as soon as we turn the key in the ignition.

Because trust is all about this ability to rely on someone or something to deliver the outcome we want, it then becomes a critical part of all our interactions and relationships, in our business and working lives as well as in our personal lives.

If the specific outcome we want is not delivered, that's when we start saying things like, "They can't be trusted," "She broke my trust," "I can't trust this to work." We've all thought this way at some point in our lives, and those thoughts are accompanied by feelings of disappointment, annoyance, bitterness, and even anger at times.

In your business, every employee, every manager, every customer, every potential customer, every shareholder is constantly going through a process of assessing whether they can trust in you, your company, and your products or your services. Can they rely on you to deliver the outcomes they want?

The bigger questions, however, are: How did they come to choose you to rely on? and How do you know what outcome they want? Let's look at the trust model next for some answers.

Something to Do

How would you define trust?

2

THE TRUST MODEL

*Trust is a key building block in the creation of a company's reputation,
and as a direct result, it's shareholder value.*
—Robert Eckert, CEO, Mattel

To understand how we choose the people we trust, we have to first get a better handle on what trust is—in simple terms.

Following my heart-wrenching experience with my son over the issue of broken promises, I started thinking about what trust is and how it breaks down so easily.

What I realized is that Lachlan formed an expectation in his mind when he heard me say we "might" go to the movies. In reality, I wasn't sure that we would have time to go, but I left it open as a possibility.

The other thing I realized was that promises are so easily made, and we make them all the time. The problem is that we don't always keep them. This is one case where good intentions do not help; you can't lean on the "But I meant well" statement when it comes to making promises. We'll explore more about promises in detail later.

I really can't recall at what point I designed this model, but I can say this: It is already changing the way people interact with each other. It is changing the way managers and employees have honest conversations. It is changing the way leaders lead their companies. It' is changing the way companies promote their products and services.

I draw the model to look like a structure with three walls.

The first wall represents our expectations.

Each brick represents an expectation we have of the relationship or interaction we are entering into.

Relationship or interaction: I use these words throughout this book. What I mean by relationship is simply a relationship with someone or a company. It could include managers with their staff, customers with customer service representatives, shareholders with a company, and so forth.

I use the term "interaction" to cover things like purchasing a product or eating a meal. It is simply every instance of us doing something with something else in which we are expecting and need some sort of outcome, and that outcome may have been promised to us in some form.

The chapter on expectations will explain more about how expectations are formed, but it includes things like previous experiences, things we've heard or seen, or things other people have told us.

Basically, each time we enter into a relationship or an interaction with a person, a company, or a product or service, we bring a load of expectations with us.

The trouble is, oftentimes we aren't aware of them, and as a result, we usually don't tell the other party what we expect.

The second wall represents our needs.

Each brick represents a need we have that makes us seek out a relationship or an interaction in the first place.

We all have needs. We may be conscious of some of them, but often we are not. When I talk about needs, I often refer to Abraham Maslow's Hierarchy of Needs, which we'll explore in more detail in the chapter on needs.

So, expectations and needs are the things we bring with us when we are entering into a relationship or interacting with a person, a company, or a product or service.

The third and last wall represents promises.

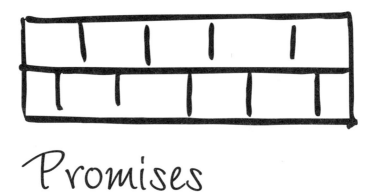

Promises

Each brick represents a promise that was made to us by the other party and drew us to that particular person, company, or product or service.

Importantly, there are two main types of promises we make: implicit and explicit.

Briefly, because we will look at this in more detail in the chapter on promises, an implicit promise could be sayings like, "Work hard and you will be rewarded." What the heck does that mean? I might think that "work hard" means working through my lunch break a couple of times a week. Someone else might think "work hard" means logging an eighty-hour workweek. Someone else might think "work hard" means meeting all the objectives outlined in their performance appraisal. On top of that, the word "rewarded" could also mean very different things to different people. One person could be expecting a bonus, another a gift voucher, or a third a day off.

The key thing about implicit promises is that they are unclear. In and of themselves, they create more expectations—and a multitude of variations from one person to the next.

Explicit promises, however, are very clear-cut; they leave no room for confusion or misunderstanding. For example, "If you complete these five key performance indicators [KPIs] by the end of June, you will qualify for a $5,000 bonus to be paid before August 31." Great! We all know what is expected and what the reward will be.

So, our complete wall ends up looking like this:

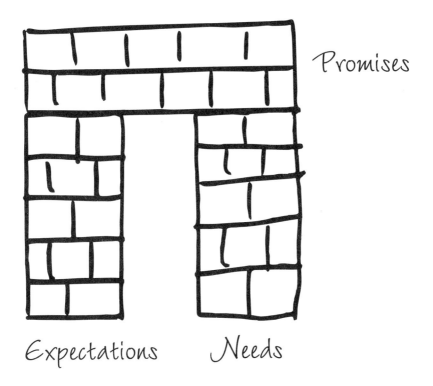

Every relationship, every transaction is based on these three elements—expectations, needs, and promises—and our decision to trust is based on the interaction of these three.

Now, the critical issue concerning this wall is that if certain expectations and needs are not met, and certain promises are not kept, the bricks start to drop out of the wall. Of course, at some point the wall will actually collapse. What I wanted to know was how.

I thought, "Someone is going to say to me in a workshop one day, 'That's not how that wall would collapse!'" So I met with a structural engineer to find out what would actually happen.

The engineer actually told me some interesting things about this wall. Here is what he said.

On the expectations wall, if you took bricks out of the top and bottom parts of the wall, like…

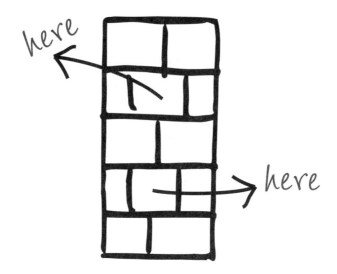

...the wall would still stand. If you took bricks out of the middle part of the wall—and sometimes you might only have to take out one from...

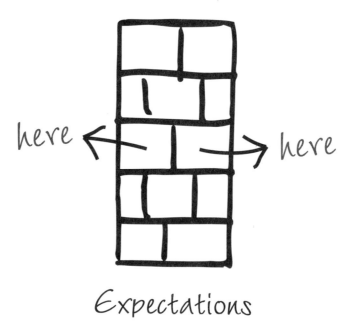

Expectations

—the wall would collapse to the left or the right.

What this said to me was that there are some expectations that are more important to us than others.

When you think about it, this is true. I may have one expectation of my manager that he not eat his smelly lunch in the office. I may have another expectation that he listen to me when I have an issue. If he eats his smelly lunch in the office, it's not a deal breaker. If he brushes me off when I try to talk about an issue, that's a big problem for me.

The same thing applies to needs. I have one need to be recognized for a job well done, and I have another need to get paid. If my manager doesn't give me a bunch of flowers for something I did, it may not be a big deal. If I don't get paid one week, I have a major problem.

The key thing to remember here is that everyone has different expectations and different needs, and each of us ranks them differently.

This is where most people go wrong when it comes to relationships: We make assumptions about what people expect and need, and we are surprised when they suddenly aren't happy with us!

When the engineer and I looked at the promises wall, he said that if you took bricks out of the center parts of the wall, like…

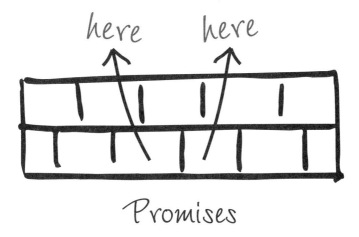

…cracks would appear in the wall before it collapsed. In other words, you'd actually be warned of its collapse! If you took bricks out of the end parts of the wall, like…

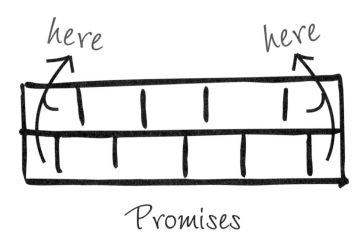

here   *here*

Promises

…the wall would collapse with no warning! In engineering terms they call this a catastrophic collapse.

What became clear was that explicit promises sit in the central part of the wall, because if you don't keep those types of promises, you hear about it! It is explicit promises that customers complain about, that staff raise with their boss in a meeting. Implicit promises sit on the outer parts of our promises wall. These are harder to have a conversation about. Think about it. If someone told you, "Work hard and you'll be rewarded," how would you then sit down with them and say, "You know that bonus I thought I was going to get…?"

So, what happens when implicit promises are not kept is that staff will just hand in their resignation and you won't even know why! Customers will just go somewhere else and won't even bother complaining to you. How often could this be happening to you?

SO, WHAT ABOUT TRUST?

When I thought about trust itself, I realized it has these qualities:

1. It is fragile.
2. It can break easily.
3. When it breaks, it is usually irreparable.
4. When we have it, it holds us together.

The best thing I could think of that represents trust is an egg. An egg is fragile. If you tap an egg, it cracks. If you drop an egg, it breaks. And, once broken, it cannot be repaired. When we cook, we use an egg to bind the ingredients together. If you were going to put an egg on the top of a structure, wanting the egg to stay intact, you would want that structure to be so stable that the egg wouldn't topple and fall, right?

The great thing about this image is that if we then represented our trust as an egg, and placed it on the relationship wall I have just described, we would end up with…

We all know the famous nursery rhyme "Humpty Dumpty," and we remember that when he falls, nothing can put him back together again, which is exactly what happens to our trust when the expectations-needs-promises wall breaks down completely.

The entire process of trusting is analogous to placing this fragile "trust egg" on a structure that balances our expectations and needs and the promises the other party has made to us, hopeful that all will remain in balance. When some of our expectations or needs are not met, or when some of the promises are not kept, those bricks start disappearing from the wall, and our trust, the egg, is in serious danger of falling and breaking.

It is on the combination of these three things coming about—expectations, needs, promises—that we choose to place our trust.

I call these ENPs, which you will read about consistently throughout this book. The wall we built is our ENP wall.

So, how do we build trust, and keep it?

Building trust is fundamentally about three things:

1. Manage people's expectations of you, your business, and your products and services.
2. Meet people's needs.
3. Keep your promises.

Sound simple? In some ways it is, but it takes awareness and understanding and consistent processes to get it right.

Much more about building trust in business will be explained throughout the book, and some practical tips and exercises are included for you in the chapters in part 3, "Assessing Trustworthiness."

To really understand the trust model in depth, though, we need to understand expectations, needs, and promises in greater detail. Read on!

Something to Do

Think of a time where you lost trust in a coworker, in a company, or in a product or service you bought. What expectations did you have, what needs did you have, and what promises where made to you?

3

EXPECTATIONS

We must ensure that our clients gain a clear understanding of
what they can and cannot reasonably expect from us.
—David H. Maister, Charles H. Green,
and Robert M. Galford, The Trusted Advisor

The *Oxford English Dictionary* defines an expectation as:

- An act or instance of expecting or looking forward
- Thing expected or hoped for
- Probability of an event

There are mathematical equations that look at "expected value" as part of probability theory, but for the purposes of exploring expectations in the role of trust, we will keep things simple.

We all have them. Every time we enter into a relationship or an interaction with a person, a company, a product or service, we have expectations. The interesting thing about expectations is that sometimes we are aware of them and sometimes not; sometimes we let others know about them, but most of the time we don't.

The key thing is that when our expectations are not met, we experience disappointment, sometimes anger. The trust we may have had in that person or business may start to slip. In fact, trust can break altogether, depending on how important our expectations were and how they were linked to our needs and the promises made.

WHERE DO THEY COME FROM?

Our expectations come from a number of places:

- Our own direct experiences with a person/company/product or service
- What others tell us
- What we read, hear, or see
- Similar experiences with someone/something (recent or past)

Let's explore each one of these in more detail.

Expectations from Our Own Direct Experiences

Each time we interact with someone or with a business (for example, as a consumer, an employee, or a manager), we form expectations about what will happen the next time we have another such interaction.

You know the saying "First impressions last." Well, that actually applies to our own expectations as well. In fact, our first impressions are often so strong that we get confused when the next interaction goes against what we first thought. This is also linked to our need for the interaction to develop into a stronger relationship.

Let's look at an example of how expectations are formed from direct experience.

Mary goes into her local bank branch to get a money order drawn from her account. She waits just a few minutes before a friendly teller serves her. She gets the money order and leaves.

Two weeks later, Mary needs another money order. She goes into the same branch and sees a long line. She has to wait fifteen minutes before she is served. The teller this time is eager to take his break, but he serves Mary because his supervisor said he needed to help reduce the line of customers. The teller is a bit gruff with Mary, but eventually she leaves with her money order.

Mary's initial expectation may have looked like this:

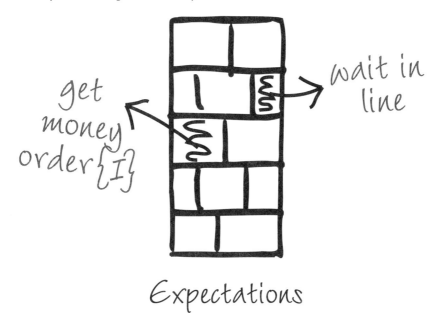

Expectations

"Get money order" is an important expectation; hence, it is marked (I), whereas "Wait in line" is not important. In fact, Mary is actually hoping she doesn't have to, but she expects it nevertheless.

Based on her first experience, however, Mary's expectations going back to the bank a second time looked like this:

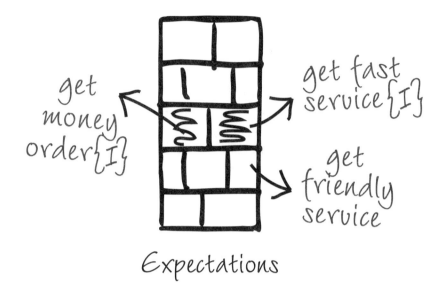

get money order{I}

get fast service{I}

get friendly service

Expectations

"Get money order" is still important, but now "Get fast service" is also important; it's even more important than friendly service, although that is still an expectation.

Are her expectations reasonable? Maybe not.

Are they logical? Yes.

Mary had an experience that she enjoyed and so she expects that same experience again.

What's interesting is that we do this all the time. We are often not aware that this is happening, but with each occurrence, our expectations are adjusted or raised and then not met.

Let's look at what happens to Mary's expectations wall:

Her ability to trust in the service she gets from that branch has been damaged. She still got her money order, so that part of the wall is still intact. She wasn't served quickly, however, and the service certainly wasn't friendly, so that part of the wall has collapsed.

Trust may not be broken, but Mary is not a happy customer, and she will begin doubting the ability of this bank to meet her expectations. She will readjust her expectations as a result whenever she has a need that drives those expectations.

Expectations from What Others Tell Us

How quickly do rumors spread? We know that as customers, we often end up telling people of our bad experiences rather than our good ones. This creates expectations in people's minds. On the upside, recommending a great restaurant to someone or giving someone the name of a potential new client also creates expectations—positive ones.

Let's look at an example.

Tom has applied for a job at a company where a friend of his works. He meets his friend David for lunch the day before the interview. "So, what's it like to work there?" asks Tom.

"Oh, it's great! They're pretty good on work/life balance, so the hours aren't ridiculous. I actually get to go to the gym before I head home, which makes dealing with the kids easier when I get there!" jokes David.

Tom may have had very little expectation of this company before that conversation, but now his expectation wall looks like this:

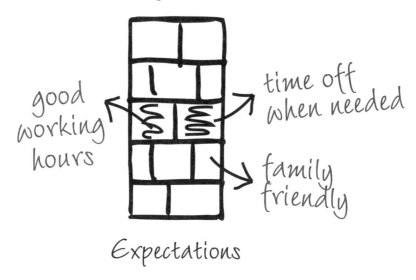

good working hours

time off when needed

family friendly

Expectations

The interesting thing to note here is that Tom has made some assumptions based on what David has said. When David said, "the hours aren't ridiculous," Tom has taken that to mean "good working hours," which in his mind could be nine to five. This, of course, may not be the case. Tom also heard David talk about work/life balance and time with his kids, so he has assumed the company is family friendly and he can get time off when he needs to. To Tom, these two aspects of the company's culture are important, and so they sit in the important section of his expectations wall.

Let's look at what could happen to Tom's expectation wall if he starts working for this company and is repeatedly asked to work overtime and can't take some time off to take his son to an open house at his new school.

As with Mary, Tom's trust is not broken, but he is not happy. We'll look specifically at expectations and trust in the work environment in chapter 14, "Trust in People Management."

Expectations from What We Read, Hear, or See

Marketing and advertising create expectations. That is one of the primary functions of these two fields. Web sites, mission statements, values, billboards, food labels, radio jingles, TV commercials, and restaurant menus—all of them create expectations.

Let's look at a specific example.

Olivia finds a catalog for a toy store in her mailbox. "Perfect," she thinks. Her son's birthday is coming up, and she spots a blue bike in the catalog that she knows he will just love. It's Saturday morning, so she decides to head off to do some shopping and will go to the toy store while she's out.

Olivia's expectation wall looks like this:

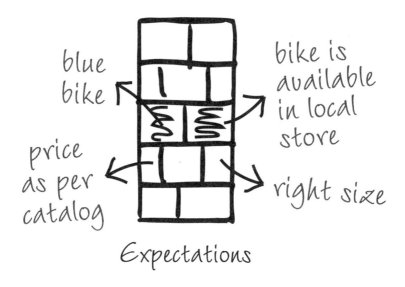

blue bike

bike is available in local store

price as per catalog

right size

Expectations

Olivia arrives at the toy store and asks an assistant where she would find the bikes. "At the back," the assistant replies halfheartedly with a wave of her hand. Olivia can find only a couple of small tricycles, however, when she goes to look.

"Sorry," says Olivia, returning to the assistant, "but I'm after this one," she says, pointing to the blue bike in the catalog. "It's for my son's birthday in just a few weeks," she adds, smiling and nodding.

"Oh, we sold out," says the assistant with a shrug.

"What do you mean? I got the catalog just this morning in the mail. You can't have sold out that quickly!" Olivia is clearly frustrated.

"You'll have to speak to the store manager, lady. I don't know what happens around here."

Now look at Olivia's expectation wall:

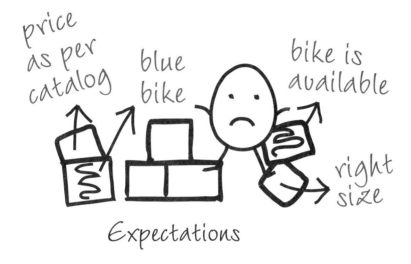

price as per catalog

blue bike

bike is available

right size

Expectations

The thing to recognize is that companies create expectations constantly in the minds of consumers, staff, potential customers, prospective employees, shareholders, directors, and managers.

Expectations from Similar Experiences

Similar experiences are probably the subtlest creators of expectations, and it may take a while for people to recognize these expectations within themselves and others. This is where generalizations take place and we can fall into the trap of writing off a person, a company, a product or service without even giving them a chance.

Here's an example.

Zac has a great job. He gets on well with the boss, and they occasionally head off together for a game of golf on a Friday afternoon. Then, one day, things change. Zac's boss accepts a transfer to another department, the new boss starts immediately, and he is a she!

Zac's never worked for a female boss before, so he doesn't know what to expect. She spends a bit of time evaluating his work and general career development and decides that Zac needs to boost his performance. She starts to scrutinize his productivity. She lets him know when she is not happy with his work, and she does it so the others on the team can hear.

One day Zac decides to confront her. "I think I'm being unfairly treated," he complains to her in her office.

"Oh, really. Well, you needn't think I'm going to take you off for golf games and pretend that your work is up to par (pardon the pun). You might have been lucky before, but those days are over," she says with her arms folded and a smug look on her face.

What do you think will happen the next time Zac ever has to work for a female boss?

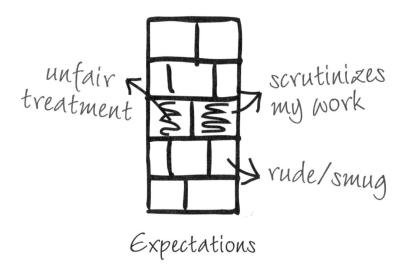

This may or may not be a fair assessment of his next boss, but he now has expectations of female bosses based on a similar or generalized experience.

Interestingly, as this example illustrates, expectations can be negative. Just as when they are positive, negative expectations affect our behavior toward the person, company, or product or service. It will often take some effort to convince someone that they can now expect something different. That's why building trust can take so much time!

MANAGING EXPECTATIONS

Expectations, as we have seen, come from different places, and they are different in each person. Is it possible to meet everyone's expectations all the time? No.

What we can do, though, is *manage* people's expectations. We will look at how you manage employees' expectations and customer expectations in part 3.

People often ask me, "How do I know what people expect?" The answer is simply, "Ask them!" That can happen one on one, through a survey, or in focus groups, for example. The point is to ask them, and then keep asking them because people's expectations change over time.

Managing expectations builds trust.

Now that we've looked at the relationship between expectations and trust, let's explore the role of needs.

Something to Do

Ask three people you have constant interactions with what they expect of you. Write them down, and let the three others know if those expectations are realistic or not.

4

NEEDS

Leadership should be born out of the understanding
of the needs of those who would be affected by it.
—Marian Anderson, African-American recipient
of Presidential Medal of Freedom

The *Oxford English Dictionary* defines need as:

- Stand in want of; require
- A requirement
- A thing wanted
- Circumstances requiring some course of action

Throughout the 1950s, American psychologist Abraham Maslow fine-tuned what is probably the most commonly known academic model of needs. We'll draw on his "hierarchy of human needs," adapted for our purposes, as we talk about needs in this book.

It is actually our needs that drive us to seek out a relationship or an interaction in the first place. Think about it for a minute. We subconsciously say to ourselves, "I need something, therefore I take action to have my need satisfied. When I have multiple needs, I search for something or someone that might satisfy some, or all of, those needs."

What type of needs do we have? Maslow describes different types of needs and groups them like this:

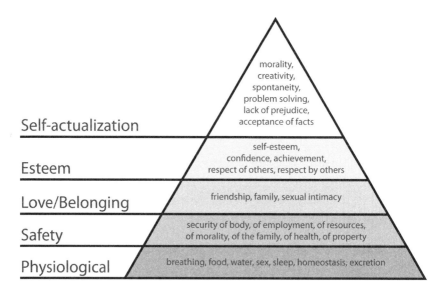

Diagram of Maslow's Hierarchy of Needs, represented as a pyramid
Source: Wikipedia

The four lower levels are called "efficency needs," and the top level is called "growth needs." Maslow's theory, basically, is that the higher needs come into focus only after all the lower-level needs are met. If the needs within a particular lower level are not met over a long period of time, all levels of need are temporarily re-prioritized, with a focus on that particular level until all of its needs have been satisfied again.

Remember, this is important to understand from a trust perspective, in which we are talking about our ability to rely on a person, company, or product or service to deliver an outcome.

What is the outcome we want? We want our needs to be met!

As we explored earlier, we also have expectations about how those needs might be met, how often, by whom, and so on.

Let's have a look at needs from both an employee and a customer perspective. We are going to use an adapted version of Maslow's hierarchy by changing the "physiological" to "physical." This shifts from the basic human needs to breathe, eat, sleep, etc., to the basic physical things we need to achieve our outcomes, such as food, transport, and technology.

FROM THE EMPLOYEE'S PERSPECTIVE

If we took the adapted version of Maslow's Hierarchy of Needs and put it into the employee's perspective, it might look like this:

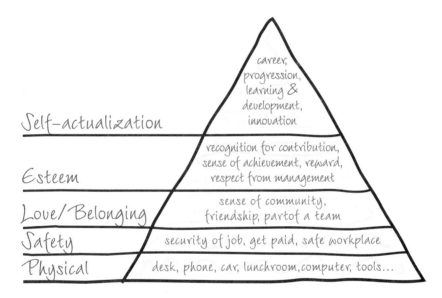

So, let's look at an example of a real-life employee.

Julia was so excited. Today was the first day in her new job. The people she had met during the interview process seemed really nice. They told her there was a real sense of family in the company, and everyone got on well together. One of the company's values was innovation, so Julia thought this would be a great place to show her creative flair on the job and be recognized for her innovative contribution.

Julia's needs wall looks like this:

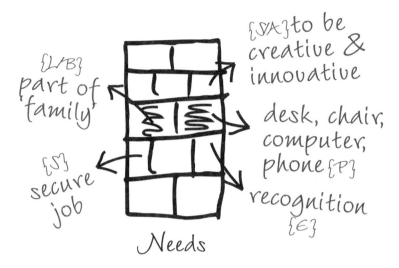

Needs

Julia arrives early and the HR manager takes Julia to her manager's office to get started.

"Hi Julia. How are you feeling? I'm really sorry, but we still haven't sorted out a desk for you yet, so you'll need to just put your things here," apologizes the manager as she points to the end of her desk.

"It's been pretty hectic and, what with the announcement of the takeover yesterday, we're all still somewhat in a state of shock. Anyway, let me show you around."

What does Julia's needs wall look like now?

Needs

Clearly, her basic physical needs have not been met at this stage, and these are pretty important at such an early stage of settling into the job. Julia now also has doubts about her job security, having heard the news of the takeover. She's not sure about being part of a family either; she doesn't know now whether or not the people she met will even still be there.

We will look at more of what happens to employee trust in chapter 14.

FROM THE CUSTOMER'S PERSPECTIVE

If we now take Maslow's Hierarchy of Needs and put it into the customer's perspective, it might look like this:

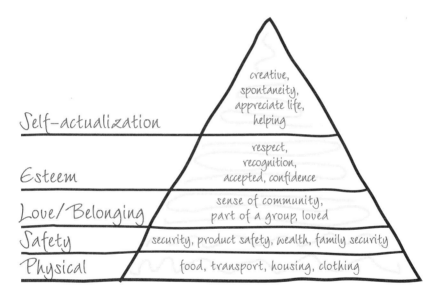

Let's look at an example of a real-life customer.

Luke decided it was time he bought himself a new car. He had just accepted a new position with his company, but it didn't include a car. He thought he'd just get something basic that would get him from Point A to Point B, but when he stepped into the showroom, something else caught his eye: the brand-new BMW 325i convertible, with retractable hardtop—in silver!

"Now that's the car for me!" thought Luke. "Looks great. Zero to 100 mph in 5.8 seconds. My boss is also a BMW driver, so that would go down well. Good solid car, too."

Luke's needs wall looks like this:

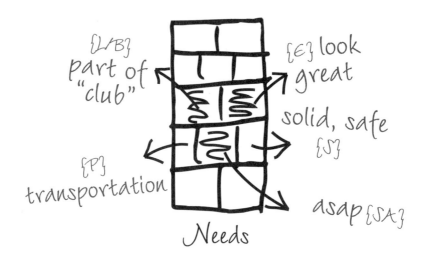

Luke is told the car loan will take a couple of days to process. In the meantime, a friend of his tells Luke that he needs an old car just to drive around town, so Luke says he could have his clunker. "Come around to pick it up next week. I should have my new car by then."

When Luke gets to work on Monday, he knocks on Gary's door and walks in with a smile. "Guess what I did on the weekend? Bought myself a new BMW 300 series convertible!"

"Hey. You should have told me you were in the market for a new BMW. I traded mine in last week for a new Bentley Continental GT. Zero to 100 in 4.8 seconds!"

Luke feels a bit flat, but after a quick chat with his boss, he rings the dealer to find out how the loan processing is going. "Oh, I'm glad you called. We've just heard that delivery of your new convertible is going to take a bit longer than we thought. Demand has been huge and there's a backlog of orders. But we will have you driving out of here in your brand-new car in around six weeks' time."

What does Luke's needs wall look like now?

Luke is now in a dilemma because he has committed his old car to a friend, which will leave him without his basic physical need of transport. Consistent with Maslow's theory, Luke will first seek to have that need fulfilled. He may not have lost trust in the dealer, but he may not be as keen on the overall "brand" now that it does not deliver his immediate need of being part of a club (especially in his attempt to impress his boss).

MEETING NEEDS

The important thing to understand here is that as human beings, we will seek out ways to satisfy our needs. Sometimes we will look to one thing to satisfy as many needs as possible because, basically, this is easier for us. For example, many people look to their employer to satisfy their needs not only for basic things like pay but also for their sense of belonging, their recognition, their sense of self, and their personal development. If some of these things are not already being met in such other places as sports clubs, family, and self, then the loss of a job can be far more tragic than if those needs were being met elsewhere as well.

As I mentioned earlier, it is our needs that drive us into a relationship or an interaction. What we must focus on in order to build trust is trying to understand what those needs are, in ourselves, and in those who are in a relationship or interacting with us.

Find ways to determine what those needs are. A good salesperson will identify the needs of a potential customer and then position what they are selling in a way that meets those needs. Apply that same practice to your own situation by asking yourself these questions:

> As an employer, do you know what needs your employees are seeking to meet through their employment?
> As an employee, do you know what needs you are seeking to meet through your employment?
> As a shareholder, do you know what needs you are seeking to meet through the companies in which you invest?

Then ask yourself, "Is this the right relationship, the right company, the right place through which to have those needs met? Is it fair to expect that? Should I be seeking some other relationship to satisfy some of those needs in order to take pressure off this relationship?"

Remember, meeting needs builds trust!

Something else to consider is who bears the responsibility for trust. If I looked to one place to have all my needs met and that was unrealistic, whose fault is it that my trust is subsequently broken? Both parties are responsible for keeping trust intact: The person placing their trust needs to be responsible for their choice, and the person making the promises needs to keep them.

Let's look now at promises, the third and final aspect of our trust model.

Something to Do

Think about what needs you have that have driven you to choose the company you work for or a recent product you bought. How well are those needs being met?

5

PROMISES

Stand up for what's right, in small matters and large ones, and always do what you promise.
—Reuben Mark, Chairman and CEO,
Colgate-Palmolive

The *Oxford English Dictionary* defines a promise as:

Assurance that one will or will not undertake a certain action

It's pretty simple, really. We all know what promises are. What we seem to have forgotten, though, is what happens when we make them and subsequently break them!

Someone once told me that he did not make promises at work. I thought that was odd. I asked him, "Do you make commitments? Do you tell people that you will have something done by a certain time?"

"Oh, yeah, sure. I guess I hadn't thought of them as promises."

Another time someone told me that she thought keeping promises was more important at home than at work. "Why?" I asked.

"Well, if you make a promise to your kid, then you try to keep it, but if you make a promise to someone at work, and you don't keep it, it doesn't matter as much."

"Do you really think so?" I continued. "Don't you think your coworkers have the same feelings as your children when it comes to the matter of trust?"

"Hmm, well I guess it might impact their ability to get their job done, or it might effect how they respond to their customers. OK, I understand now!"

So, let's take a look at the role of promises, considering the two different types we talked about earlier—"implicit" and "explicit." Remember that although expectations and needs are what we have going into a relationship or an interaction, it is the promises being made to us that draw us into that particular relationship or interaction with a person, company, or product or service.

IMPLICIT PROMISES

We might call implicit promises waffling half-promises. I refer to them as the "Let's do lunch" promises. Often they can be well meaning, but they're deliberately kept vague so we don't feel bad when we don't get around to them.

They are also the things we don't really say but strongly suggest in the wording we choose or the look we give, including body language and facial expressions.

This means that implicit promises can be embedded in things like a company name, a company's brand, the packaging of a product, the way a salesperson or customer service representative behaves, or the way a manager looks at his or her staff, to name but a few.

As we saw earlier in the discussion about the trust wall, when implicit promises aren't kept, the wall can collapse suddenly, without warning. This is analogous to us getting to the point where we think, "I can't be bothered with this any more," and we just leave without even saying anything.

Let's look at an example of implicit promises.

Rachel has just been laid off from work and given a substantial amount of severance pay. She is looking for a new investment adviser and sees an advertisement in her local paper for AAA Investments. This is what the ad said:

> Are you tired of financial advisers that look after their own future before yours? Call AAA Investments today.

Their impressive logo, printed in blue and gold shows a friendly person shaking hands with a middle-aged man with a smile on his face.

"Looks like these people are friendly," thinks Rachel. "Like they will have my interests at heart and will look after my future and my goals. And with a name like AAA Investments, how can I go wrong?"

Here's what her promises wall looks like (the implicit promises that she believes have been made to her):

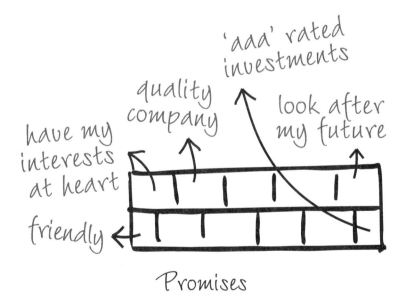

Rachel picks up the phone at nine o'clock Monday morning and calls AAA Investments. No one answers. Rachel tries again a few minutes later, and the girl who answers the phone sounds a bit gruff.

"Hmm. Maybe they're not as friendly as they make themselves out to be," Rachel muses. Nevertheless, she makes an appointment for later that morning with Ted, one of AAA's top advisers, and decides to withhold judgment.

When she walks into their offices she is a bit surprised. The carpet has a few worn patches and the chairs in the waiting room don't match. "Let's hope their investment process is better than their decorating skills," Rachel says to herself.

No one is at the front desk, and when Rachel rings the bell, a young girl calls out from a room in the back, "Be there in a minute!"

"Must be the same girl who answered the telephone," thinks Rachel. "They should definitely do something about her."

Ted comes out to the reception area, looking a bit frazzled, and he shakes Rachel's hand as he turns and leads her into his office. As she sits down, he pushes a pile of papers out of the way to clear a spot on his desk. He runs through some options for her that sound as though they would meet Rachel's financial and lifestyle goals, but some of his suggestions make Rachel feel a bit nervous.

"I'm not sure that I want to be that aggressive with my investments at this stage," says Rachel.

"Hey, these are solid investments, Rachel, and sometimes you have to take risks to get the reward!" Ted protests.

Rachel decides not to commit to anything that morning and makes a quick escape.

Let's have a look at what happened to Rachel's promises wall after her encounter with AAA Investments:

Amazingly, many companies appear to be unaware of the important link between implicit promises and a person's ability to trust in them. It often comes down to the simple things. In this case, the use of AAA in the business name, the blue and gold branding and the friendly faces in the ad may be clever from an overall marketing and positioning perspective, but not if the office has threadbare carpet and the staff are rude and pushy. The huge disconnect between the implicit promises and the actual delivery breaks down the wall.

The most important thing to realize about implicit promises is that they create different expectations in different people's minds. They are open to interpretation, and this can be dangerous from a trust perspective. What Rachel took from the advertisement may have been different from what the next person might take from it.

I said earlier that broken implicit promises will not always collapse the wall instantly; we often give people the benefit of the doubt and offer them another chance. How many chances we give will depend on the expectations and needs that are linked to the promises, which we will explore later.

In Rachel's case, she has other options to consult for investment advice (a point we will look at in chapter 15, "Trust in Branding and Marketing"). It is unlikely she'll go back and complain to AAA; in fact, she just won't go back there at all!

Implicit promises and their breakdown are hard to measure. Why? Because people are less likely to complain or raise an issue over an unmet implicit promise than they will over an unmet explicit promise.

The implications of this are huge for businesses. In part 3 we will look at some specifics about the role of promises and how to build trust.

EXPLICIT PROMISES

I refer to explicit promises as the clear-cut, "I know what I'm going to get" kind of promises. They create certainty. They leave no room for interpretation. Consequently, they encourage trust, especially where they directly meet a need.

Unmet explicit promises will form cracks in the wall before a complete collapse. How long those cracks are there will depend on how quickly the person or company responds. That may be minutes, days, weeks, months, or years. Again, this also depends on the linkages between the person's expectations and needs and the explicit promises made to them.

Let's look at an example of explicit promises.

Dean is about to sit down for his performance review with his boss. Reviews are supposed to be done every six months according to the employee handbook, but Dean's is already three months overdue.

His key performance indicators (KPIs) were pretty specific, as was the corresponding reward, and Dean is feeling pretty confident that he met them. In particular, two of them were:

- By end of September, develop and roll out training on Product Y (Dean completed his training across relevant parts of the business.)

- By end of October, complete concept development of Product X for consideration for launch (Dean submitted his concept plans a month early.)

In his position description it states that if Dean met his KPIs, he was eligible for a 20 percent bonus (percentage of base salary).

Let's have a look at Dean's promises wall (explicit promises made to him):

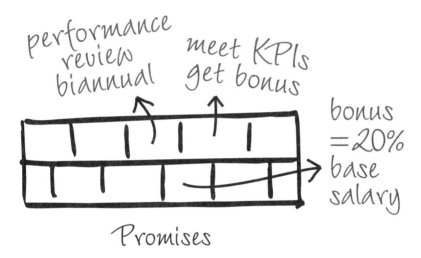

When Dean met with his boss he was told that although he had met his KPIs, senior management hoped he would have stretched himself more and gone "above and beyond."

On top of that, Dean was also told that the company had not performed well enough financially to allow them to pay the stated bonuses. Instead, a share of a lesser pool would be given to those who had contributed most to the company over the year.

Now let's look at Dean's promises wall:

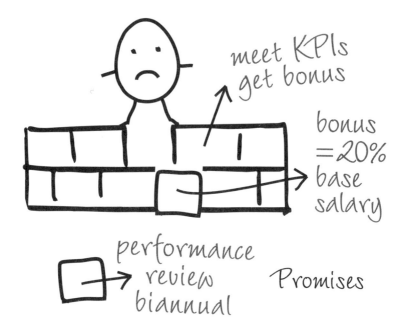

Although there are cracks in Dean's promises wall, he intends to take this up with HR and the CEO if he has to: This is just plain wrong. Dean's discussions with senior management will determine whether the wall collapses or the cracks are repaired.

KEEPING PROMISES

Keeping promises is the most basic form of maintaining trust. It displays reliability, integrity, honesty, and empathy—all qualities pertaining to trustworthiness.

I referred earlier to the interviews my company conducted in 2006 with six hundred people across Australia. We asked them to tell us which of the following was the most important thing for a business to do to build trust:

- Manage expectations of consumers
- Meet consumers' needs
- Keep promises that are made

Sixty-five percent of the respondents said that keeping promises was the most important way for businesses to build trust. As a business, we make promises in all sorts of forms. For example, promises are made in:

- Branding
- Advertising
- Web sites
- Values statements
- Mission statements
- "Who we are and what we do" statements
- Employment contracts
- Employee handbooks and policy manuals
- Work for hire agreements
- Shareholder announcements
- Meetings, To Do lists, agendas
- General business communications

Scary, isn't it! How many promises are out there that you are not keeping?

How many are implicit and thereby causing disengagement of staff or contributing to customer retention issues?

Remember, keeping promises builds trust!

Now, let's bring all three components together!

Something to Do

List three promises you've made to someone (implicitly or explicitly) that you will now make sure you meet!

6

CONSTRUCTING AN ENP WALL

You can't have success without trust. The word trust embodies almost
everything you can strive for that will help you succeed.
—Jim Burke, former chairman and CEO of Johnson & Johnson

In this chapter we're going to look at how expectations, needs, and promises—the three core components of any trusted relationship—all fit together. We'll also look at the role that time plays in building and breaking down trust, and what this means for business.

Let's start by going back to a specific example we looked at earlier, and throw some extra light on it.

Olivia finds a catalog for a toy store in her mailbox one Saturday morning. Her son's birthday is coming up, and she spots a blue bike in the catalog that she knows he will just love. She decides to head off to do some shopping and will go to the toy store while she's out.

We know that her expectations wall looks like this:

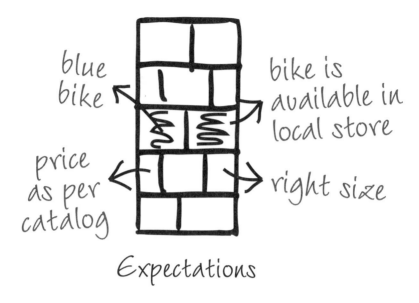

Expectations

What we didn't know earlier was that the catalog said a storewide sale would begin Saturday morning, and that Olivia's son had been nagging her for a bike for more than six months.

So, what does the rest of Olivia's ENP wall look like?

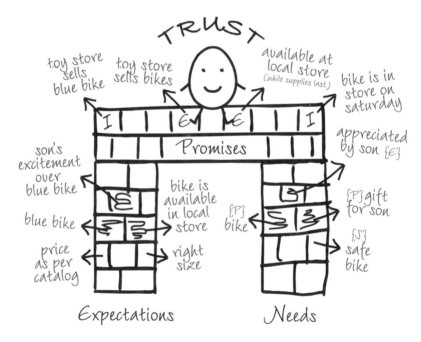

Expectations   Needs

If we look at this bit by bit, we notice that Olivia's needs are basic: In this situation, she needs a gift for her son. That gift needs to be a bike, to satisfy her son's nagging, and the bike needs to blue, his favorite color. Olivia also has a need to be appreciated by him, for her son to be pleased that for his birthday she bought him something he wanted.

This last need translates into an extra expectation that her son will be excited about the bike. The shaded needs are Olivia's most important ones, so they sit in the section of the wall that is most critical.

As a mother, Olivia also has a basic need for the bike to be safe, but this is not as critical to her as some of the other needs. (Remember, we are all different. Some of you, for example, might be thinking that safety should be her number one need. This is a key thing to be aware of, then: we place different levels of importance on our needs. We cannot assume that one person's needs are the same as our own. That's how we begin to break down trust.)

It is Olivia's needs that made her notice the bike in the catalog. If she did not need a bike, she may not have even noticed it. If her son's birthday was not coming up, she may not have even looked at the catalog at all.

Notice the promises made by the toy store. They have made both implicit and explicit promises. Interestingly, the availability of the bike is explicit, as evidenced in the comment "while supplies last," but by using a picture of a blue bike in the catalog and advertising a sale, the toy store is making an implicit promise that they will have bikes—and probably blue ones.

Now, let's recall the rest of Olivia's story. She arrives at the toy store and asks the assistant where she would find the bikes. The assistant gestures toward the back of the store, but Olivia can find only a couple of tricycles. When Olivia returns to the clerk and points to the picture of the blue bike in the catalog, the clerk just shrugs and says they must have sold out.

Olivia is clearly frustrated and incredulous, but the clerk merely suggests that she speak to the store manager.

So, now that we are looking at the whole wall, let's work out what has happened to Olivia's trust in this toy store. Remember that we define trust as the ability to rely on a person, company, or product or service to deliver an outcome.

In this case, we are looking at Olivia's ability to rely on the local toy store to be able to sell her a blue bike in time for her son's birthday.

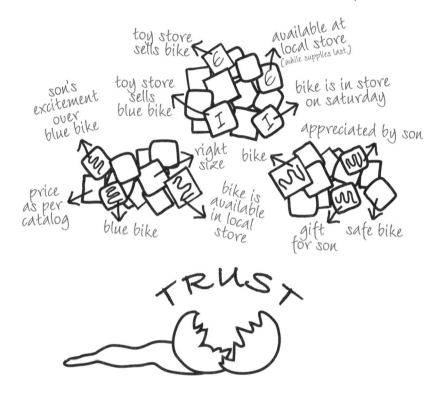

There are five important observations to note here.

- Olivia still has the same needs, she just can't have them satisfied by the local toy store that day, which is why the needs wall broke down. What will she do? She can ask whether they can order the bike from another location so that she can pick it up in time for her son's birthday, although their attitude has not encouraged Olivia to try that. Her other alternative is to go and find another store that can sell her a blue bike in time. We will always seek out ways to satisfy our needs.

- While one of Olivia's needs was to get a gift for her son, and she could have bought something else for him from the store, it would not, in her mind, have satisfied her other need for appreciation by her son. We will always seek out ways to satisfy a combination of needs first before we choose to compromise.
- The explicit promises have not been broken: The toy store chain does sell bikes. Olivia's local store sells bikes, just not the one she wanted. There was no stock so, technically, that promise was not broken. Nevertheless, technically keeping explicit promises but, at the same time, not meeting expectations and needs will still break down trust.
- The implicit promise that there would be a blue bike in the local store on the day the sale started was broken, so the promises wall collapsed as a result. Broken implicit promises can drag you down, even if you keep explicit promises.
- Olivia's expectations of her local toy store have not been met. Unmet expectations instantly create new ones.

So, the big question is, Will Olivia shop at this toy store again? The answer will depend on a number of factors.

1. Her needs— Will she need to buy another toy for her son?
2. The importance and urgency of her needs—If they are both important and urgent, she may still go to that particular toy store to fulfill those needs, but because her trust was completely broken, she will avoid going there as much as possible.
3. The availability of another toy store nearby.

Something I want to stress about our needs is that they drive us into relationships and interactions. But here's the rub: The greater the need, the quicker trust can be built and even rebuilt. The more choices we have available to us, the easier it is to seek another provider to fulfill our needs.

Let's take Olivia's example a little further into the year. Christmas is coming up, and she wants to buy her son a Spiderman action figure (her son has been nagging her again!). If:

1. The need is important enough she will seek to have it fulfilled.
2. There is another shop nearby that sells Spiderman action figures, and the local toy store also sells them, she will go to the other shop first.
3. There is another toy shop that is farther away, and her need is urgent (that is, it's Christmas Eve and the shops are about to close), she will most likely go to the local toy store first, but she will do so begrudgingly.
4. There is no other alternative, she will go back to the local toy store, but her expectations will be managed down. Based on her previous experience, she may expect an unhelpful assistant and that the store may or may not have the action figure.
5. The toy store advertised Spiderman action figures in a catalog with the same "while supplies last" caveat, she may not believe them this time around.

Because the experience of broken trust is painful, we do all we can to avoid placing ourselves in that situation again. We all do this. It is natural for human beings to avoid pain. What is important to understand is that your employees do this, your managers do this, your customers do this, and your shareholders do this. If you break down their trust, they will try to avoid any situation where it can be done again.

In the example above, Olivia's wall collapsed completely. This does not always happen. I talked before about cracks appearing; sometimes the wall might collapse on one side, but trust does not completely break. Nonetheless, there is work to be done to rebuild trust. The complexity comes in when we look at situations where there are multiple expectations, multiple needs, and multiple promises. The key thing that comes into play, then, is time.

THE TIME FACTOR

What happens to trust over time? Can you build trust quickly? Can longer-term relationships hold up and bear "mistakes"? What great questions! Let's find out.

Because we are going to explore the questions above, this example is longer than the others. (Just managing your expectations!)

Ben was looking for his first job after graduating from high school. He read this ad, which is pretty simple and doesn't say much, in the newspaper:

> Help wanted. Enthusiastic, hard worker needed for small family-owned business. Call Jim.

When Ben answered the ad, Jim told him to show up at 8 AM on Monday. His job would be to help them box up books and contact the delivery company when all the orders for the day had been filled. He would be paid $10.00 per hour.

Ben's ENP wall looks like this as he starts his new job:

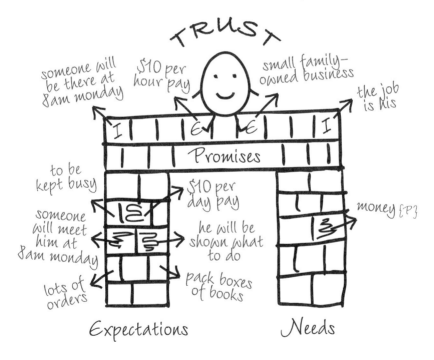

The special observations to note about Ben's wall at this point are:

- Ben has just one basic need—money. It's the reason he sought the job. Ben does and will have other needs, but at this stage he is unaware of them.
- Ben has some expectations about being shown what to do and that there is plenty of work to do. Because this is his first job, he has no reason to believe otherwise, so his ability to trust comes easily.
- The promises conveyed through the ad were pretty basic; again, Ben has no reason to believe they won't be kept.

Over time, Ben proved to be a good worker, so Jim gave him more responsibility. Ben began answering the phones, taking orders, and packing shipments; he had even started helping Jim improve the company's Web site. Ben loved having more responsibility, and the variety of the work was really important to him.

Jim and Ben, as well as Jim's daughter, all got along really well. They often ate lunch together, and sometimes the three went out for a drink after work.

Jim suggested to Ben that he might want to take a course in Web design so he could redevelop the company's Web site and maintain it for them.

Jim also raised Ben's wages to $15 per hour. Ben felt that Jim had really taken him under his wing and that they had developed a good friendship.

Now Ben's ENP wall looks like this:

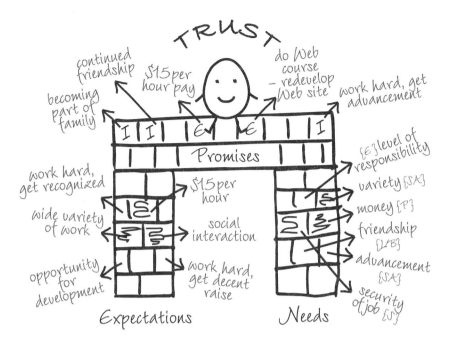

The special observations to note about Ben's wall at this point are:

- Ben's previous expectations have changed because the earlier ones, such as "to be kept busy" and "someone will meet him at 8 AM Monday," have been met and are no longer relevant.
- Ben's needs are now more complex. He is relying on this job to meet a range of needs across the needs spectrum—responsibility, advancement, and friendship, among others.
- The implicit promises are building up now and are based on behaviors and events that have been happening. Because Jim has delivered on his promises, has met the expectations, and has fulfilled the basic earlier need, Ben has no reason to believe that that won't continue. His trust is well placed at this stage, and Ben is happy and performing well for Jim's business.

One day, Jim took his lunch break with one of the other workers and didn't ask Ben to join them. Soon afterward, Jim's daughter left the family business to travel overseas. Jim caught up with Ben only about once every two weeks or so. The business was growing, so there wasn't as much time for the two of them to socialize.

Jim decided that Ben needed to be working on Web site maintenance pretty much full-time, so Jim hired other people to answer the phones and handle the packing and delivery management. He gave Ben another raise—to $17 per hour—but Jim couldn't afford to give him more than that because he had others to pay now as well.

Jim told Ben he would continue to pay for his professional development and would send him to some more IT courses. Jim could see that his business needed someone to handle a range of IT-related tasks, and he liked Ben and wanted him to do that work for him.

Now Ben's ENP wall looks like this:

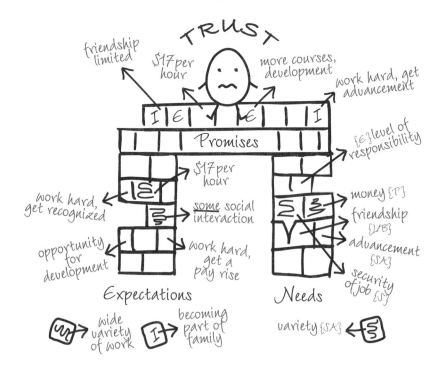

The special observations to note about Ben's wall at this point are:

- One of Ben's needs, his *need* for variety, appears no longer to be met now that Jim wants Ben working primarily on IT and maintaining the Web site.
- Likewise, Ben's important *expectation* for a wide variety of work has not been met. Because variety is one of the key things that drive Ben, he will either seek it out here with Jim or (quite likely) leave, finding another employer who can deliver that for him, as well as deliver on his other needs.
- Some of Ben's expectations have adjusted along the way, such as the one for social interaction. If things get to the point where there is no social interaction at all, and no sense of friendship between Jim and Ben, the wall is likely to collapse altogether, as this linked an expectation, a need, and one of the remaining implicit promises.
- Jim's implicit promise of Ben's becoming part of a family has dropped out of the wall. The other implicit promise has adjusted to the friendship being limited.

The combination of these changes has caused a few bricks to drop out of the wall and has created a sense of unease for Ben. He is not as happy working for Jim as he once was, and his ability to trust in Jim to deliver the outcomes he, Ben, wants is now wavering.

Get the picture? In any given relationship or situation, our ENP wall changes over time. What often happens is that we are unaware of this and the impact it has on our ability to trust, to rely on the other person to deliver the outcome. On top of that, the outcome we want changes over time as well!

Everything is subject to change, and all three sections of our ENP wall are affected. As expectations change, we learn how to manage them and to adapt. But there will be times when we can no longer accept the state of the relationship. We become more aware of our needs as soon as one or more of them are not being met. The pain that we feel is actually an awakening, an awareness, which spurs us to seek fulfillment of these "new" needs wherever we can get them met. Promises being made to us can change too. A change in a person's behavior can create a shift in implicit promises, and that flows on to what we believe we can expect in the future, and that may also affect a need.

In a longer-term relationship, if one or two expectations are not met, that isn't usually a deal breaker. It may cause some cracks in the wall, but not a complete collapse. When a relationship is new, however, there may be just one or two expectations, so if those are not met, it has much more impact on the person's or persons' ability to trust.

The key to maintaining any relationship is to communicate each party's ENPs. If cracks begin to appear in the wall, and the other party is unaware of that, it is likely they will continue to do things that break the wall down even further.

I want to clarify a point here that a number of people have asked me: Whose ENP wall are we talking about when we look at these examples?

WHOSE ENP WALL IS IT?

Each of us chooses to trust others and to enter into relationships and interactions with them every day. We do it subconsciously most of the time, but after reading this book, you will probably become much more aware of your choices and what your ENPs are in each case.

In all the examples we have been talking about so far, there was another ENP wall. In the case of Ben, his employer, Jim, also has an ENP wall. Jim would have had needs that drove him to advertise the job that Ben applied for. He would have had expectations of the person he employed: how that person would work, how that person would behave, and how well that person would perform. Ben would also have made promises to Jim, both implicit and explicit.

This is where things get a little tricky. When Ben feels the need for variety, and Jim has a need for an employee focused on IT issues and the company's Web site, what results is actually a clash. Why? They are each relying on an outcome from the other, but the commitment—the promise—to deliver may not be there. Herein lies the critical need for openness and honesty in communication, together with an understanding of what is in danger of breaking down—TRUST!

WHAT DOES THIS MEAN FOR BUSINESS?

Everything I have talked about and shown you has huge implications for anyone who is

- Leading a company
- Managing people
- Working in a team
- Working as an individual for someone
- Creating and/or building products and services
- Selling products and services
- Delivering products and services
- Buying products and services

If you are thinking, "Well, that's pretty much everyone on this planet," you are right!

So, if we understand how trust breaks down, do we also know how trust gets built up? Yes, we do! Keep reading!

Something to Do

Choose two people you interact with regularly and take some time to communicate your ENPs with them—today. Write down their ENPs.

7

HOW TO IDENTIFY TRUST

You don't need to like someone to respect them—trust is similar.
—Karnig Momdjian, Director, KSM Link International

This chapter is really just going to touch on a few points that have come up over the years as I've studied the concept of trust. Some of these points have been particularly enlightening for people, who will often tell me months later that these ideas about trust have changed the way they think and behave. That, for me, is the whole reason I do what I do! Let's see what you think.

"TRUST" IS DIFFERENT FROM "RAPPORT"

The *Oxford English Dictionary* defines rapport as:

Harmonious and understanding relationship between people

Feeling of being in harmony

Many people use the words "trust" and "rapport" interchangeably, but I believe they are two different things. Nevertheless, one does contribute to the other.

As we know, trust is our ability to rely on a person, company, or product or service to deliver an outcome. How do we choose to rely on one person over another? To a large extent, that is where rapport comes in.

Rapport is basically the process of creating a sense of being in sync with or on the same wavelength as the other person. Techniques—often subconscious— such as maintaining eye contact, matching body language, dressing in a similar way, and speaking in a similar tone are used to create a sense of harmony and understanding between two people.

From a trust perspective, what that does is form expectations in our minds. For example: "OK, so this person is a bit like me; therefore, I can expect her to interact and behave in a similar way. There should be no surprises. I can rely on her."

Rapport may also meet a basic need for safety. For instance: "I feel safe around this person. He seems to have my interests at heart."

Rapport may also meet a need for friendship, a sense of belonging.

The process of building rapport also includes such aspects as being open and transparent, as well as caring and empathetic. As you'll see in chapter 12, those are all qualities of a trustworthy person.

So, building rapport is a part of leading people to a decision to trust someone or something else, but "rapport" is not "trust."

"TRUST" IS DIFFERENT FROM "APATHY"

I asked a friend of mine once what toothpaste he used. "Colgate," he replied.

"Do you trust Colgate toothpaste?" I asked. His answer threw me a curve ball.

"I don't know if I trust it, or if I'm just too lazy to change to another brand."

Now there's something I hadn't thought of before. Is there a link between trust and apathy?

We know that trust is our ability to rely on an outcome that meets our expectations and needs, and that we seek out relationships, products, services, and experiences that promise us that those expectations and needs will be met. Would we continue to use a product, such as toothpaste, that did not meet those criteria?

Let's explore this in more depth. When I buy toothpaste, my trust wall looks like this:

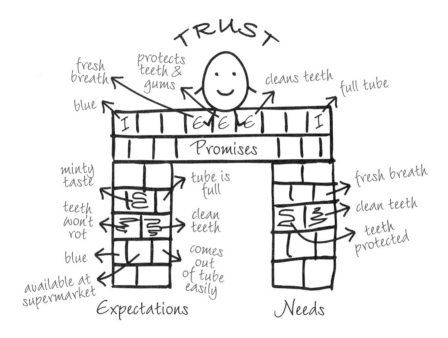

If I found that

- The tube was half empty
- The toothpaste tasted like soap
- The toothpaste was black
- The toothpaste caused my teeth to rot

I would not continue to buy that brand, even if I had to drive some distance in order to buy another brand. Why?

Because:

1. One of my most important needs was not met.

2. Four of my expectations were not met.
3. Two of the manufacturer's implicit promises were not kept.
4. One of the manufacturer's explicit promises was not kept.

So, if all the criteria were met, I would continue to trust in my brand of toothpaste. In fact, I will continue to trust it for as long as my expectations and needs remain the same and the promises made by the toothpaste manufacturer continue to meet those expectations and needs.

APATHY OR TRUST?

Let's have a look at trying another brand. If all my expectations and needs are being met, will I try another brand? I don't believe so.

What, then, might cause me to try another brand?

1. A new product that raises my expectations over and above my existing toothpaste.
2. A new product that highlights, through a new promise, another need I have but am unaware of. For example, if another brand markets itself as making teeth whiter, I might think, "Yeah, I want white teeth!"

I start to consider the alternative. Why? I have a new need for white teeth and an expectation that I'll get them from the toothpaste I use. Let's have a look at my trust wall now:

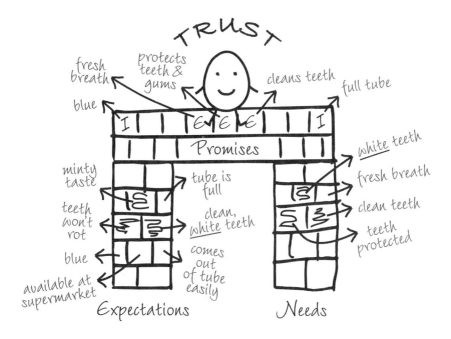

I begin to question whether or not my existing brand can deliver on my new expectation and need. I may begin to lack trust (that is, I am not sure I can rely on it to deliver on my expectations and needs) in my existing brand and decide to try the new brand to test it out.

I may just jump to the new brand, or I may choose to try it out for a period of time and assess whether it really does live up to its promises. I may also go back and test the old brand to see whether there is a significant difference.

Trust enables us to become lazy or apathetic about a product, service, or relationship, but only until an alternative is produced or we become aware of one that either raises our expectations or highlights a new need.

In the chapter on marketing and branding in part 3, we will look at this in more detail.

TO "TRUST" IS DIFFERENT FROM TO "LIKE"

In the survey Entente conducted across Australia, I asked these two questions: "Would you deal with someone you liked but did not trust?" and "Would you deal with someone you trusted but did not like?"

The results revealed that, on average, only *one in ten* people would do business with you if they liked but didn't trust you.

Interestingly, if you are dealing with women, only one in twenty will deal with you if they like but don't trust you. With men, on the other hand, one in five will deal with you if they like but don't trust you.

What this tells us is this: If you are spending your time trying to get your stakeholders to like you, you really needn't bother! Spending time getting them to trust you will deliver much greater results, especially if your leaders, managers, staff, customers, or shareholders are women!

One of the most common mistakes we find in a range of areas in business is the effort devoted to getting people to "like" each other and to socialize and to getting the customer to think we are "nice."

Granted, the sense of belonging is a need that we all have to varying degrees, but the purpose of a business is fundamentally for an individual or a group of people to produce an outcome (product or service) for the end user. That is, the end user must be able to trust in that individual or group of people to deliver the outcome.

In what aspects of business is this critical?

- When you are hiring a new employee: Are you hiring someone you like, or someone you can trust to do the job?
- When you are working with your colleagues: Does liking them help when they don't deliver the report you need for your next client meeting?
- When you are advertising your products or services: Does liking the advertisement help if the product or service delivers a bad experience?
- When your salespeople are meeting customers: Does liking them help if they are not delivering results?

Trust is the key element to business success.

It is far more critical to understand how to build and maintain trust than it is to get people to like you.

TRUST IS A GIFT

To have earned someone's trust is one of the greatest gifts you can receive.

How often do we think of it that way though? My observation and experience both tell me that most people in business do not appreciate the value of someone's trust. Unfortunately, what you don't appreciate, you don't take care of; consequently, trust is often inadvertently and "accidentally" broken.

Think about it: If someone decides to come and work for you, what they are saying is, "I trust you—the company, the leaders, the manager—to meet my expectations and needs, and I believe you will keep the promises you have made to me." That's a gift.

Likewise, the leaders and managers are giving their trust to the employee, to the customer, to the shareholder, to the supplier—to meet their expectations and needs and to believe that the promises made will be kept.

When someone trusts you, they are giving you a gift, a precious gift. They are placing their trust on top of their expectations of you, their needs they are looking to you to fulfill, and the promises you have made. Their ability to function effectively, their growth, dreams, future, happiness, safety, and sense of self could be dependent on you.

Trust is a gift; treat it with care.

Now that we have a better understanding of what trust is and what it is not, let's get a handle on different types of trust that we all encounter.

Something to Do

Name a time when you tried to get someone to like you rather than trust you. What happened?

8

TYPES OF TRUST

We're never so vulnerable than when we trust someone—
but paradoxically, if we cannot trust, neither can we find love or joy.
—Walter Anderson, political scientist and author

Some people will give their trust quite openly and willingly, and others take more time and are wary. Why is that?

The answer is simply that there are different types of trust, and I will touch on a few of them in this chapter. It's important to be aware of the various types because it will affect your ability to understand and build trust with various people.

BLIND TRUST

I'm sure you know people who just blindly trust others; you may even be like this yourself. Why do some people do this, and what are the consequences?

I believe that, to some extent, blind trust is personality driven. In fact, I've started exploring the links between personality preferences and ENPs.

Although there is more work to be done on this, some general observations can be made about blind trust.

- People who deal more in principles than in facts may be more likely to trust first and ask questions later.
- People who are driven to achieve and create may be more likely to jump into a situation blindly.
- People who are caring for and always thinking of others may be more likely to blindly trust.

Though it might seem like a wonderful thing to be so trusting, what we often find is that people who blindly trust are often left disappointed. Why?

People who act with blind trust may not have spent time considering their ENPs. That is, they should ask themselves: "What am I actually expecting from this situation? What do I need and what are they promising. Does all this stack up and deliver the outcome I want??"

It is not necessarily in their nature to think in this way, so, as a result, their trust can be broken down. What can happen thereafter is that their expectations change, and they may become more skeptical in certain situations rather than remaining blindly trusting.

On the upside, these people will put themselves out there, trusting first, and they can often embrace change and be more flexible and innovative, even if the original outcome they wanted was not delivered.

SKEPTICAL TRUST

Just as we know people who blindly trust, we also know people who are very wary and skeptical about whom they trust. You may be like this yourself. Again, why do some people do this, and what are the consequences?

My general observations about this type of trust include the following:

- People who deal in facts and seek clarity may want everything to stack up before they trust someone or something.

- People who need to experience things for themselves and to have proof may be skeptical until they are satisfied that a situation is OK
- People who need to know the bottom line—What does this mean for me?—could appear to be skeptical about trusting you until you can show them that such trust is well placed.

Though skepticism may seem to some as negative, these people are often proven right in that they choose carefully who they trust, and they know why they chose that person, company, product, or service over another. They may be clearer about what they expect and need and will explore the likelihood of the promises made actually being met.

The downside of this type of trust is that in its extreme—namely, a fear of trust—it can prevent people from reaching decisions, from taking advantage of opportunities, and from achieving outcomes.

The chart that follows summarizes these two types of trust for easy reference:

Type	Characteristics	Upside	Downside	Need to...
Blind Trust	• Deal in principles not facts • Driven to achieve and create • Caring and thoughtful of others	• Get things done • Embrace change • Innovative • Flexible	• Often disappointed • Not clear about the outcome wanted	• Spend some time thinking about the outcome and the ENPs before blindly trusting

Chart continues on next page

Type	Characteristics	Upside	Downside	Need to...
Skeptical Trust	• Deal in facts not principles • Driven to experience and find proof • Need to know bottom line	• Get the desired outcome • Clarity of decision • Resourceful	• Often slow • May miss opportunites • Not flexible	• Spend some time focusing on ENPs rather than ALL the facts to speed up ability to trust

The Middle Ground

Can some middle ground be reached between blind trust and skeptical trust? Sure. I only highlighted these two extremes because we've all seen them and we've probably played a part in them at some stage.

Neither type is right or wrong, but it is interesting to observe and now understand a little more about what drives us, and what the consequences could be.

SITUATIONAL TRUST

Is it possible to trust someone in one situation but not another? Absolutely!

This is something that confuses all of us from time to time. Just because you were able to trust someone as a fellow employee does not mean you can instantly trust him or her as a manager. Just because you can trust a company to provide one service does not mean you can instantly trust them to provide a different service. Just because you can trust a CEO to build a new company does not mean you can instantly trust her or him to maintain the company.

What happens is that we believe we can trust someone, or something, and then we try to stretch the trust out across other situations. When we do this we

- May not consider what it is we expect in the new situation
- May not think about what our specific needs are in the new situation

- May not find out if they are able to promise or commit to delivering on the expectations and needs

Let's have a look at a real-life example.

Sarah has been in her role for two years now at the call center. She fields more than the average number of calls each day and has built a great rapport with the customers over the phone. There has been just one complaint from a customer, and that was really a misunderstanding.

The call center management's ENP wall looks like this (that is, how they currently trust Sarah):

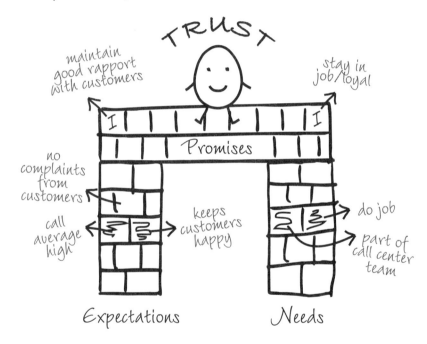

Sarah's manager has been promoted to work in another department, and Sarah has been told that the company's executives would like her to move into the management role. It will mean supervising a team of ten and dealing with any complaints that cannot be handled by the call center staff. It will also mean a salary increase, which Sarah is very happy about! She has accepted the job and told them she will do her best. There has been no real handover, however. Sarah has been told her job description will get sorted out later; they need someone in the role urgently.

The call center management's ENP wall now looks like this:

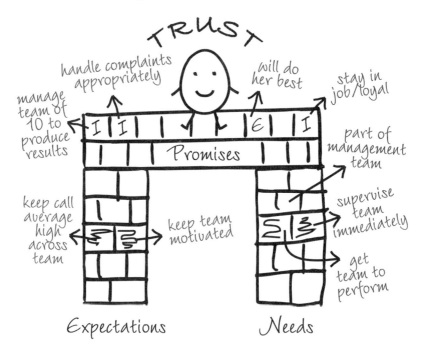

Sarah has had no experience managing or supervising a team, and she has not had to handle complaints for two years. As a result, she does not perform well in the new job. In fact, the call averages slip, the team is not motivated and does not respect Sarah as a manager, and a number of complaints escalated to the managing director level.

The call center management's ENP wall ended up like this (see top of next page).

Was Sarah "bad at her job," or were the call center management's expectations of Sarah too high, their needs out of her reach to deliver on? Sarah did her best, as she explicitly promised, but in the end, the company could not trust her in a management role at this time. The management also did not recognize that in order for Sarah to live up to their expectations, they might have needed to provide her with some management training.

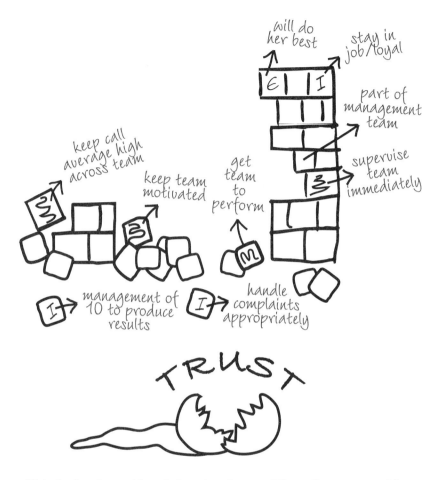

This is the downside of situational trust. The call center could trust Sarah in her role as an operator, keeping the customers happy, but not in a different situation—namely, managing a team to do what she, as an individual, had done so well.

What we need to be mindful of is how often we stretch our trust across to a situation that may or may not be appropriate or fair. Always keep in mind the ENPs and consider each situation separately to avoid disappointment!

REFERRED TRUST

We have all seen and participated in referred trust, but do you know why? Because it works! Simple examples of referred trust are when we ask someone, "Do you know a great restaurant east of the city?" or "Do you know anyone who might be interested in my products?" and they pass on those details.

People in sales know the power of referred trust better than anyone, and we can all benefit from it. On the surface it is simple, but it does have some more complicated aspects to it that are worth being aware of.

Let's have a look at how it works and the role situational trust plays with referred trust.

You (A) have situational trust with someone (B).

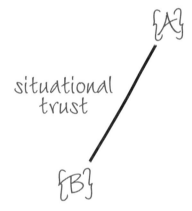

(B) has situational trust with someone else (C).

By situational trust in these examples, I mean there is trust in (B) and trust in (C), but in a specific instance, as we discussed earlier. I'll talk about why this is relevant later.

You (A) want to get to (C). The best way to get to (C) is through (B). Why? Because you want to deal with someone you can trust! If you had moved into a new area and were looking for a doctor, you would ask someone (B) who you trust and lives in the area, "Which doctor do you go to?" rather than directly going to (C), who is a doctor. Why do we do this? Because

- It saves time
- It cuts out some of the hassle of trying to find (C)
- We believe it eliminates some risk
- We benefit from referred trust

So, you (A) now have referred trust in (C) because (B) referred him or her to you.

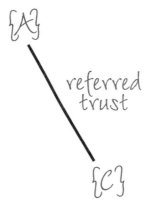

In its simplest form, trust flows one way on each line (see diagram next page):

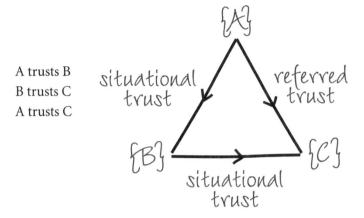

A trusts B
B trusts C
A trusts C

Situational trust becomes relevant in two special instances: (1) when you (A) trust (B) in a certain situation, but ask for a referral that is not linked to that situation, or (2) when (B) gives you a referral where the situational trust is not clear.

Let's take a real-life example.

You (A) have situational trust in Louis (B) because you play soccer together. After a game one Saturday, you ask Louis whether he knows of a good cabinetmaker because you want to renovate your home office. Louis gives you the name of a guy (C) he met at his son's soccer camp who said he was a cabinetmaker. Louis has not seen any of (C)'s work.

The interesting thing that happens when we trust someone is that we often adopt blind trust in accepting what they say and the people they refer us to. Why? Because they have not let us down in the situation or situations in which we trusted them before.

If you hire the cabinetmaker (C) to work for you, based on referred trust from Louis, and you are satisfied, your trust in Louis actually gets stronger. If, however, you have a bad experience with (C), that can have a negative impact on your trust in Louis.

Who is responsible for the referred trust? You (A), Louis (B), or the cabinetmaker (C)? In cases where we have a bad experience, we usually blame everyone else but ourselves. If we are to accept responsibility for our trust and to make sure we give it solely to someone deserving of it (that is, some-one we believe will meet our ENPs), what should we do differently?

You could:

- Ask Louis if he has ever used a cabinetmaker
- Ask Louis if he knows a cabinetmaker and has seen any of their work
- Ask the cabinetmaker to show you some of his work
- Ask someone who has hired a cabinetmaker

The more specific you can be about your expectations and needs, the easier it is for someone to refer you to someone who can deliver on those.

I said earlier that the trust in this case was flowing one way. In what instances does it flow both ways?

If you (A) are looking for someone (C) who might be interested in you or your products or services, you need trust to flow both ways on each line.

Here's an example to illustrate this concept.

You (A) have a suite of information management solutions that have been helping your clients perform better by having ready access to infor-mation about their businesses. Your client, "Beinformed," is very happy with the work you have done for them recently.

You have a new business continuity plan (BCP) process and need some clients to buy into it. Beinformed has a BCP, so you ask their chief oper-ating officer, Joshua (B), if he knows anyone in his circles who could be interested. Joshua (B) knows one person in particular who could use your help, and because there is a two-way flow of trust, Joshua is happy to refer you to Richard (C).

Joshua and Richard have known each other for a few years and are members of a business association. When Joshua calls Richard to let him know you will be contacting him, he says, "Great, thanks for that. I've been hassled about getting our BCP done." The situational trust is flowing both ways between the friends.

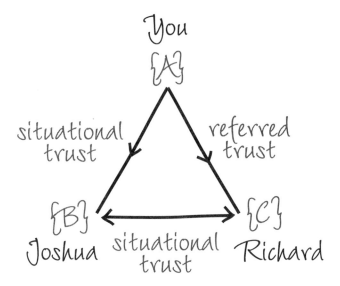

When you contact Richard, the referred trust is also flowing both ways. This two-way referred trust will backfire only if you do not deliver on the ENPs Richard has. In that case, it will backfire on you as well as on Joshua. It is critical that you understand and value this trust triangle in any situation where you are seeking and giving referrals.

When would this be relevant in business? Some examples would include any time you are:

- Looking for referrals for more customers
- Seeking new suppliers or distributors
- Asking existing employees to find new recruits for your business
- Asking colleagues what it's like to work in another area of the business
- Looking for a new product or service as a customer

Now let's look at part 2, actual case studies of how trust is built in the workplace.

Something to Do

Think of a time when someone referred you to someone or to something and it was not right. What went wrong? (Hint: What were your expectations and needs, and did you articulate them?)

TRUST IN THE WORKPLACE: CASE STUDIES

9

WHY TRUST IN BUSINESS?

*Total return to shareholders in high trust companies was
almost three times higher than [in] companies with low trust.
—Watson Wyatt, "WorkUSA 2002: Weathering the Storm:
A Study of Employee Attitudes and Opinions"*

When I started studying this whole concept of trust and its importance in how we interact with each other, a few people asked me if I thought it would fly in a business world. They objected with comments like: "Oh, that's warm and fuzzy stuff," or "I'm really only interested in the bottom line."

Call me strange, but I found these comments pretty shortsighted, and they themselves indicate the lack of understanding about what trust really is. They got me to thinking, though: Can a business run without trust? What would such a business look like? What would the difference be if the business did have trust?

Six different areas create the core where expectations, needs, and promises play out in any business, no matter what its size or industry. These six areas are:

- Leadership
- People Management
- Marketing and Branding
- Sales
- Customer Service
- Compliance and Governance

I believe common ENPs apply to each of these areas. This is based on years of consulting experience across businesses, interviews with CEOs and senior executives, discussions with consultants and specialists in different fields and industries, and research into articles and books on trust in business.

What became evident to me is this: Building trust drives direct and indirect improvement in what I call the 3 R's of trust:

Results
Retention
Relationships

The best way to demonstrate this is to go on a journey with a couple of companies to see what they have done to build trust and to learn what their outcomes were.

10

TRUST IN ELLA BACHE

To be trusted is a greater compliment than being loved.
—George MacDonald, Scottish author and poet

I first heard Karen Matthews, CEO of Ella Bache Australia, speak at a net-working event, and I think she mentioned the word "trust" about fifteen, times! I thought, "I need to meet this lady."

Karen has done amazing things at this world-renowned skincare prod-ucts manufacturer, and I saw value in having her share some of her insights. I interviewed Karen in January 2007, and she talked about the role of trust in three key areas of Ella Bache's business:

1. As an employer with their people
2. In their salons with their customers
3. Between the head office and the franchisees

What follows is a transcript of our conversation.

1. Tell me about the role of trust with your people?

Trust starts with the leader. The key to being a great leader is:

- Being true to what you say—you have to walk the talk.
- [Being] totally honest about strengths and weaknesses, which a lot of leaders shy away from. It's easy to deliver good news, but it takes courage to give honest feedback.
- Being "real." This encourages trust and fosters a culture of honesty. Decision making becomes richer and more powerful, as people are not afraid to say what they think.
- [Having] no hidden agendas. When you are open, people know where they stand. When there are hidden agendas, businesses become fraught with fear.

At Ella Bache we are true to our values, and most of them require trust. Our values are:

- Honesty—requires and creates trust
- Creative—requires trust to feel free to be creative
- Energy—having energy in what we do
- Results driven—being clear about the outcomes and delivering on them
- Brave—requires trust to be able to make decisions

We assess our people in their performance reviews on a 50/50 split. Fifty percent of their assessment is based on their performance against their objectives. The other 50 percent is about how they lived up to the values.

I believe that when you are in a company that really is an extension of its values, people thrive. We have a lot of fun and laughter here, but that is coupled with drive to produce results. People who want to work here just for the fun don't last. Likewise, people who are just results driven and focus only on the numbers don't last either.

You need to be true to all the values, not just some of them. That's what people expect when they come to work for an organization, so, as a leader, you have to deliver on that. One of the things that we always do is involve the people in the business. I give them updates on the business and its plans, and we collectively look at areas for improvement. They are aware of our progress against plans, our financial results, and we survey the staff each year and discuss any issues that come from that.

Importantly, we involve everyone, not just management. There is a real sense of connectedness and responsibility. How can you expect your people to be creative and make appropriate decisions if you are not giving them the information to work with?

2. What about trust in the salons with your customers?

Let's face it; customers have to trust in the salon and our products. They submit themselves, their bodies, their faces to be treated by a beautician—that takes trust.

Our business is not about beauty. It's not about products. It's all about relationships. The salon owners and beauticians build rapport and trusted relationships with their customers. We want them to keep coming back.

We are building a profitable business based on repeat and referral business and are growing almost completely from our core now. If that is not a demonstration of trust, I don't know what is.

3. Tell me about the relationship between the head office and the salon owners, your franchisees.

It's interesting. We are asking people who are passionate about their business, and beauty, to invest in Ella Bache. They absolutely need to trust us and trust the brand. They invest $250,000 to fit out an Ella Bache salon, so it is a significant investment for these people. What they need and expect from us is that they can achieve the business propositions.

The model is structured in such a way that we demonstrate trust in our business and the brand by only making money after they do.

Right from the initial inquiry to become a franchisee through to [the] actual setup stage, we are there with them. We give them guidance, and we follow through on what we say. In order for them to trust us, they need to experience us doing what we say we are going to do, and we need to trust that they are going to do the same. If we did not follow through at the early stages, they would have doubts right from the start about their ability to trust us.

We then stay in touch with them to assess how we are going. We run feedback sessions with the owners. We survey them, asking them questions about Ella Bache as a company, and we then take the feedback [to heart] and continually find ways to improve.

Personally, I make sure I get to each salon three times a year—Australia wide. On top of that, I either visit or talk to three salons per week to stay on top of what is going on.

Like the staff feedback, if you are not listening, you destroy trust.

4. What effect has trust had in the Ella Bache business since you came on board?

I came into Ella Bache in 1999. My background was retail, Myer, in buying, and marketing in the fashion area. I was really drawn to the Ella Bache brand—its rawness, [its] "cool" brand personality. It has guts, and that appealed to me.

I could really relate to the brand culture and saw Ella Bache as an extension of me and my values.

When I started in 1999, we were doing $12 million in revenue, had 260 salons, [and] sold product in 34 David Jones stores and 17 Myer stores.

I knew I needed to make some tough decisions. I wanted to build a company that stands for something. I think there are too many businesses that have too many words and not enough action. So, I started to call it like it is, and by 2002 we were doing $9 million in revenue, had 200 salons, and sold product through 34 David Jones stores. We pulled out of Myer for brand protection. Although our revenue came down, our profitability went up.

In 2007, we did $20 million in revenue, still had our 200 salons, and sold through 34 David Jones stores, and our profitability has increased.

Now we are clear about who we are, how we do what we do, what look and brand we want to display. We have taken our people and our salon owners on the journey with us, and we are growing from our core—every dollar of growth is profitable.

Trust is like blood in your veins.

Lots of people talk about it, but few actually live and breathe it. I get annoyed with leaders and businesses that throw around the word "trust" but they don't define it and then behave in a way that demonstrates that [lack of definition].

Businesses need to make it real, sustainable. A real leader builds trust and creates a sustainable business. Anyone can walk into a business and be a hero in five minutes. The real proof is when you can mold a business, really listen, and apply it, and produce the results.

I want to make sure we are always:

Displaying and living with high integrity
Not compromising who we are
Applying our values

What I love about Karen's story is that she followed the trust model: managing expectations of the staff and salon owners, meeting their needs, and keeping the promises that were made.

She also demonstrates the qualities of a trustworthy person in the way she leads the company.

- She is open about herself
- She speaks the truth with her staff and salon owners.
- She is true to herself, finding a place where she feels she belongs.
- She made some tough decisions and had the guts to take the business backward to take it forward.
- She cares about her staff and salon owners and listens to them.

Now let's go to a very different type of business, with some fantastic results!

Something to Do

Consider how much of your business is repeat business? Referral based? If you consciously began to build trust—that is, begin to understand the ENPs of your customers—how much do you think you could increase your business by?

11

THE "FANTASTIC" TRUST STORY

Trust takes time to develop. But you can lose
it quicker than you can make it.
—Trevor Seymour, Partner Brentnalls NSW

Peter Draper has a fascinating story to tell about the complete turnaround of Fantastic Furniture in Australia. He agreed to include our February 2007 interview in this book. It truly is a fantastic example of trust in the workplace.

What follows is a transcript of our conversation.

1. Tell me what the state of Fantastic Furniture was when you bought it.

Fantastic Furniture was started by two ex-outdoor furniture salesmen in 1989 with only $8,000 of equity. During the next six years they grew the business to a turnover of $36 million, plowing back everything they earned into the business. They commenced manufacturing their own furniture in 1992 and were quite innovative in their methodology. However, during 1995 and early 1996, Fantastic Furniture had sustained substantial losses due to theft, lack of tight financial controls, poor staff morale, and poor management procedures.

In March 1996 the directors had no alternative but to appoint an administrator to the company. I believed the fundamentals of the business were good—they were selling good furniture at low prices to a lower socioeconomic group and had a good formula. With the right people at the helm, I was convinced that we could turn the ship around. So I gathered together a chartered accountant and ex-banker friend of mine, Peter Brennan, and one of the founding directors of Freedom Furniture, Julian Tertini, and we bought the business in May 1996.

The administrator closed a number of stores including all stores in Melbourne, and we were left with six company stores, one franchised store, and the factory at Smithfield that manufactured lounges, metal furniture, and pine furniture.

Peter Brennan looked after the company's finances, Julian Tertini took charge of the retail, and I took responsibility for the manufacturing. I had no experience in manufacturing at all, having a real estate/financial services background, but I knew how to treat people and how to motivate them to perform.

The relationship with the company's bankers, CBA, was about as low as it could get, and all they wanted was to get their money back. However, as part of the deal with the administrator, we insisted that the bank maintain the line of credit that was in place.

Shortly after I took responsibility for the factory, I found that there was considerable theft taking place and so undertook a detailed investigation to find the source. Those responsible were immediately removed from the company. This included some senior staff, so I found myself having to step in and run the factory on a daily basis. The factory had approximately 115 staff and staff turnover of around 60 percent.

I found that the suppliers to the factory were very wary but nevertheless supportive and hopeful that the three of us would [turn] the company around and that they would have the opportunity to recover much of their losses.

Creditors received only a few cents on the dollar, due to the state of the company and the losses that were sustained. They would have received nothing if the company had been liquidated, as employees' unpaid benefits and the CBA debt would have taken preference.

2. What were the expectations and needs of the people in Fantastic Furniture when you arrived on the scene?

[Because] the administrator had laid off many staff, particularly in Melbourne, and most of the staff were unskilled, they were naturally fearful of losing their jobs. They had already been informed that the company had not been paying their pension contributions, which amounted to $440,000, and they had pretty much accepted this loss. They were angry and upset. They felt betrayed by the previous management and owners, and rightly so.

There were a number of other striking issues [regarding] the staff, too many to outline here, so I'll just talk about my personal experience with the manufacturing side of the business.

There was a very strong "us and them" attitude between management and the factory staff. One day—I couldn't believe it—one of the only remaining management staff stood beside me at a mezzanine window looking out into the factory and said: "They're just a bunch of animals. I don't know how you expect to get anything out of them. You should just close the factory and import the furniture [from China]."

"Funny, I don't see any cows or horses or dogs or cats. All I can see are my fellow human beings who are simply wanting a satisfying job with financial security," I replied. It gave me an insight into how these people were used to being treated, so their expectations were probably pretty low. But they had a lot of needs that didn't look like they were being met.

The restrooms were absolutely horrifying with filth and graffiti. The lunchroom was dirty and had bird dung on the chairs and cockroaches running around the floor. There was sawdust and dirt lying on top of anything that had not been moved in the last month. The manufacturing and assembly areas where cloth was handled was almost what you could call clean—it had to be [because] they were handling fabric-covered sofas.

If you were going to the restroom, you had to see the store man to collect your sheets of toilet paper! The problem was, he was not always in the store, so if you were in a hurry, you had to go and look for him! He actually metered it out according to how many sheets you thought you might need. The story was that this had to be done to stop staff from clogging up the toilets with toilet paper and to stop them from stealing it. Unbelievable.

That's an example of what was going on. We had a lot of work to do to change their expectations and meet their needs.

3. How *did* you manage and meet those?

There was obviously a total loss of trust by staff. There was little or no trust held by suppliers who were living now in hope that Peter, Julian, and I could make a go of getting the business up and running again, so they wanted cash up front, which put high cash flow demands on us.

But the very first thing we did was to pay all outstanding staff pension contributions and to provide proof to staff that this had happened.

Again, I will refer here only to my experience with the factory. I felt that I had to demonstrate that we were serious about the business and that we were going to rely on the staff to help us in this new journey to success. We needed to trust them as much as they needed to trust us.

I met with [the] remaining section supervisors and leading hands and we identified some things we could do together to make immediate changes to improve working conditions. These included:

- Cleaning and repainting the restrooms and reinstalling toilet paper holders
- Cleaning and repainting the staff lunchroom
- Cleaning the whole factory from one end to the other
- Disposing of any redundant machinery, fabrics, and other stock
- Servicing all remaining machinery
- Replacing any damaged or broken machinery
- Cleaning up the outside grounds

- Looking at waste and seeking ways to reduce it
- Investigating our manufacturing procedures to get rid of inefficiencies

We also agreed that we would review productivity, some of the working environment issues, and the basis of pay and working hours. In the sofa section of the factory they could and were manufacturing approximately forty-two sofas per team per day. They needed to make forty-eight per day with the same number of team members just to break even.

We decided we would operate as a separate profit center and that we would need to make a profit on every item of furniture we made, albeit that we only had one customer—the retail division of the company.

The team came to understand that the retail division was not going to be forced to buy from the factory, but retail would only buy from them if they were the best supplier: that is, best quality, best service, best delivery, and most importantly, best price.

Now they had a challenge.

Within one week, all of the points above were completed including painting. We let the staff chose colors and styles—consequently, we ended up with a big green GT stripe down one wall of the lunchroom! But it was theirs. They chose it. We did what we could to include them in this new direction the business was taking.

I made one of my duties inspecting the restrooms several times a day. Within twenty-four hours of the cleanup and painting, the men's restrooms were completed flooded due to toilet rolls being jammed down the toilet bowls, graffiti depicting previous management being hung, drawn, and quartered appeared everywhere, and feces was smudged over the walls. The female restrooms were not quite as bad, but still shocking.

I immediately had all the restrooms cleaned, called the painters back and had everything repainted, and informed the staff that this was totally unacceptable behavior and that they were really only spoiling their own facilities. Their friends and coworkers really wanted to be able to use clean restrooms.

I told all the staff in a factory meeting that whoever was doing this needed to know that they would not beat me on this issue as all the rest of the staff had a right to clean facilities, and I would not let a few people spoil the needs of the rest.

The amenities were damaged again, but to a much lesser degree. This time the women's restrooms were the worst, with urine, feces, and blood smeared on the walls. I took up a bucket and a mop and disinfectant and went into the ladies restrooms to clean them myself.

About six women came up right away and insisted that I stop cleaning, and said they would do it. I asked, "Did you make the mess?"

"No," they replied.

So I said, "Why do you think you should clean it up if you didn't make the mess? No, this is the responsibility of management." I went ahead and spent a sickening three hours cleaning the women's restrooms.

That was the last time the restrooms were ever left dirty. All the staff came to appreciate that management cared about them.

There were numerous other issues that arose from time to time, but my approach was always to apply a very personal touch and to show that management would now listen to their needs and that they were appreciated and respected as important members of the Fantastic Family.

4. You also listened to the staff on the shop floor. Tell me what happened there? Why do you think it made a difference?

My management team decided that we would have meetings with staff in each section of the factory and that we would discuss productivity, pay, and hours.

So the process started. One of the first groups I met with was the staff in the fabric handling, cutting, and sewing area. We all sat on the floor in a circle and started to discuss issues. However, I found myself doing the talking and that many staff had their arms crossed and were obviously not going to be part of this discussion.

I pushed staff to tell me what was wrong, and finally I was told, "This meeting is a bloody waste of time." Another staff member said that if I wanted to downgrade their pay and increase their working hours then I should just get on and do it and let them get back to work.

I tried to assure them that things were now different, and they needed to give me a go. I pointed out all that had already been achieved, and I found that the supervisors came to my defense and said things like: "Hey guys, he is OK, right. We got our pension; we got our lunchroom back like new; we got our restrooms fixed; we got new equipment and all the crap lying around has been tossed. So, hey, enough of this negative stuff. Put him to the test. Let's just see what comes of today."

When I informed them that what I wanted to do was to see how we could afford to pay them more and reduce working hours at the same time, they all laughed and said, "Yeah, sure you do."

Then one woman burst out and yelled at me: "They never listened. I have been asking for wider sticky tape for two bloody years so I can layer more fabric, cut more layers, and increase productivity, but they have never given it to me and I am sick and bloody tired of all of you! You are full of bullshit, and I've had enough of all this crap!"

I looked straight at the man who had previously called them "animals" and told him to immediately go to the hardware store and buy the sticky tape that the woman wanted. He said, "OK, I will do it later."

I said, "You will do it NOW." He made excuses like he didn't have his car at work so he couldn't go. So I threw him the keys to my car and told him to go and buy the sticky tape. I remained calm but firm, and we had somewhat of a staring match. There was silence, as everyone was wondering what was going to happen next. He finally got up, walked out of the factory, and came back with wider sticky tape and thrust it at the woman.

That afternoon everything changed. We had an amazingly productive meeting, with staff volunteering all sorts of great suggestions and ideas. The next week sofa production went from forty-two per team per day to fifty-two per day per team. We were now above break even.

5. What promises did you make, and how did you keep them?

We promised to have regular meetings with all staff, but that I would meet with supervisors every Monday morning. At that Monday meeting we would look at the work schedules and all staff issues. I told them I would address their issues and fix them if I could, but if I couldn't, I would explain why I was not going to attend to a particular matter.

Staff were encouraged to tell their supervisors if they had an issue, and they did. As a result, some staff suggestions about the production flow saw us rescheduling the way the production line operated; we moved to a "just in time" method of production.

We moved to a piece rate pay (they were paid per item they built), with the award as the safety net. I kept my promises and they responded. Productivity crept up to fifty-six per day per team over the next four months.

Because Fantastic Furniture was making promises to its customers, we changed the way we handled quality control and "fix ups." Staff accepted that failure in quality control was their individual responsibility and that they needed to make each item of furniture so we could tell where the fault lay if a product failed. If a product was returned with a fault, it went back to the team that made it and was fixed before any new sofas were produced by that team that day.

We moved to a faster, more reliable, and cheaper method of finished product shipment to the retail stores, and we produced product to stock so that stores could now tell a customer they could have their new sofa within days instead of weeks. Sales increased in retail as a direct result of these changes.

I promised that floor staff could go home when they had finished their daily production requirement. This proved to be one of the most motivating things introduced to the factory. Production went to over sixty sofas per day per team, and production staff were down to working a thirty-two-hour week. The average staff member was now earning about 1.25 times the award wage.

6. What was the time frame in which you turned the business around?

We actually turned the business around in ninety days. There were areas where the company was still bleeding, but we had stopped all the major hemorrhaging and could see that we had a path to profitability. We then needed to develop systems and procedures, grow sales, and develop and improve staff performance to sustain it.

Despite all that we were doing, I was still put back in my place one day about six or eight months after I had taken up running the factory. Charlie, one of our tougher supervisors, said when I asked how he thought everything was going, "Same shit, just different flies." I realized I still had a long road in front of me.

7. By the time you did what you set out to do, what had happened in terms of results, retention, and relationships?

My partners and I had originally set ourselves a target that there would be a major event at the three-year mark. That would be listing the company on the Australian Stock Exchange (ASX), or the purchase of another associated business, or the sale of the business.

We floated the company on the ASX in 1999, just three years and four months after we took it over. We had retail stores in New South Wales, Australian Capital Territory, and Victoria, and the factory was by then very profitable. We were able to produce sofas cheaper than retail could either buy locally or import from China. The cheapest two-seater sofa at that time retailed for $249, and we made money in the factory, plus our normal margin in the retail division.

The sofa production had at that point reached around seventy sofas per team per day, with the same number of team members as when we started out. In fact, one of the teams had managed to produce ninety-seven sofas in one day—a major milestone they were aiming for!

From a results perspective, in the factory we had reached a net operating profit margin of 6 percent before tax, which for this type of manufacturing is very healthy.

From a retention perspective, in the factory we had moved from a staff turnover of nearly 60 percent in 1995 to less than 1 percent in 1999. We ended up with a waiting list: We had staff wanting their brothers and sisters, aunts and uncles, and cousins to get a job in Fantastic's manufacturing arm!

The Fantastic lounge factory is now the largest manufacturer of sofas in the southern hemisphere.

From a relationship perspective, the internal relationships among the teams had improved significantly, and between staff and management there had developed a deeper respect that clearly was nonexistent before.

Although we didn't understand what trust was in the way you and Entente speak about it, we did discuss practical ways we were going to go about gaining the trust of staff, and we definitely set out to build it in the only ways we knew how.

Trusting relationships with your staff is an absolute essential to any business's success. In my opinion, if you ignore it, you will fail.

What I love about this story is that the strategies and processes that were put into place were simple. Building trust is not complicated, but it does take time. It also takes careful consideration and persistence so that a company's senior managers can show their staff they can rely on the business to produce the outcomes they want, to meet their expectations and needs, and to keep its promises.

The other thing I love about this story is that Peter, like Karen Matthews, demonstrated all of the qualities of a trustworthy person as he led this change.

What I find most disturbing is that we just don't see enough of this truly inspiring behavior in business. What I do see, instead, is this:

- Fear of making the wrong decision
- Favoritism, as in meeting the needs of a select few while breaking trust with the many
- Lack of understanding of the role of trust in enhancing performance
- Myopia, with businesses treating the symptoms and not getting to the real cause of many of their issues—a breakdown or lack of trust

What people in the business world can be doing to counteract those trends is this:

- Understanding the expectations and needs of their stakeholders
- Checking on what promises are being made to their stakeholders and how well they are being kept
- Determining just how much trust they do have with their stakeholders
- Building trust proactively by managing expectations, meeting needs, and keeping promises

How, practically, do we do this? Some answers lie in the following chapters, where you will dive more deeply into the six areas of business I mentioned earlier—leadership, people management, marketing and branding, sales, customer service, and compliance and governance.

I have asked five other business professionals to write about the role of trust within their area of expertise. Each has share with you their thoughts in their own way, which means that some of the styles of writing will be a little different. I have made comments at the end of each of the chapters, exploring where the trust model applies or the qualities of a trustworthy person have been demonstrated.

In keeping with managing your expectations, let me disclose that I have written the chapter on compliance and governance, given that I have worked in that arena now for more than fifteen years.

Chapters 13 through 18 include some tips, checklists, and questions to help guide you in your venture into the world of trust. Let's lay the groundwork, however, by first looking at trustworthiness in some detail.

Something to Do

What courageous thing will you do to build trust in your business, or in your team?

PART 3

ASSESSING TRUSTWORTHINESS

12

WHO CAN YOU TRUST?

The only relationships in this world that have ever been worthwhile and enduring have been those in which one person could trust another.
—Samuel Smiles, British author and biographer

What constitutes trustworthiness? How do we know who to trust and who not to trust? These are old questions, and there are lots of answers out there concerning this topic.

As with the ENP wall, I have come up with a simple way for you to remember the core qualities of a trustworthy person, and some techniques you can apply, both to yourself and to others, in a business sense.

TRUSTWORTHINESS AND ENPS

We need to start with the correlation between trustworthiness and ENPs. Anyone is worthy of your trust if they

- Find out what you expect of them

- Find out what you need
- Promise to deliver on your expectations (or manage your expectations) and needs
- Deliver on their promises
- They are also worthy, however, if they
- Tell you if they *cannot* meet your expectations and needs
- Refer you to someone or something that can help you

Why would these last two points also constitute trustworthiness in a person? You obviously couldn't trust them to produce outcomes in any situation for which they have told you they cannot meet your expectations and needs, but you could trust them in a different, appropriate situation because you know they are not going to promise something they cannot deliver.

This is particularly important to apply to yourself: If you want to be worthy of anyone's trust—that is, you want them to trust you, to rely on you to deliver the outcome they need and expect—you need to either deliver on ENPs or explain that you cannot.

QUALITIES OF A TRUSTWORTHY PERSON

Based on years of research, I have come up with a list of what I consider to be the core qualities of a trustworthy person. To make them easier to remember, I have correlated each pair of qualities to a part of the body.

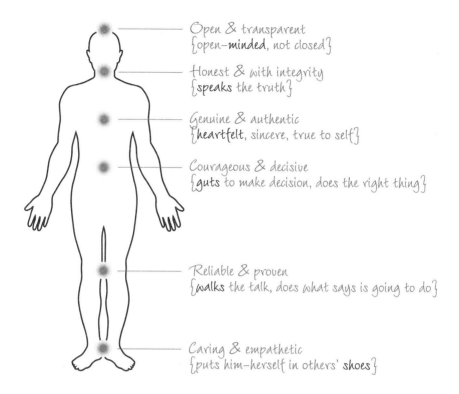

Open & transparent
{open-minded, not closed}

Honest & with integrity
{speaks the truth}

Genuine & authentic
{heartfelt, sincere, true to self}

Courageous & decisive
{guts to make decision, does the right thing}

Reliable & proven
{walks the talk, does what says is going to do}

Caring & empathetic
{puts him-herself in others' shoes}

Let's take a look at each pair in more detail.

1. Open and Transparent

This pair of qualities points to the head. Why? Because this is all about remembering to always be open-minded and allowing others to understand what is going on inside our head.

Being open and transparent is about being open to new ideas or things that may be different from your own thinking. It is about being open about yourself—who you are, and what's going on inside you. This enables people to know and connect with you, and it creates more clarity about what people can expect from you.

Someone who is closed is a person who does not share much about him- or herself, brushes off other's ideas as nonsense, and does not allow others to get close.

Shall we look at an example?

Rob approached his colleague Anthony to take a look at some new plans for the office. Anthony had a thumping headache, but he kept that to himself. As he looked over the plans, he didn't agree with one of Rob's assumptions.

"Nope. Won't work," said Anthony as he waved Rob and his plans away. Open and transparent? I don't think so.

What could he have done differently? When Rob approaches him to look at the new plans for the office, Anthony could say something like this:

"I'll take a quick look now, Rob, but I've got a splitting headache, and I'm not sure I'll do your plans justice. I'd like to take some time to have a better look later. Is that OK?"

Then, as he looks over the plans and finds that he doesn't agree with one of Rob's assumptions, Anthony could say, "Hmmm. Interesting assumption. I wouldn't mind finding out what's behind that. Can we catch up when I'm feeling better to talk it through?"

Open and transparent? Absolutely. I know some people will object, "I don't want everyone knowing what's going on with me, especially when I'm not feeling a hundred percent. That's personal, and it's none of their business." That's fine, but what happens is that those things show up nevertheless in the way we behave, our body language, and so on, and that can cause confusion about what others can expect. It is much easier to be open about such things.

The chart that follows is a short summary of this pair of traits:

Open and Transparent	
Is	**Is Not**
Being open about yourself	Being closed and secretive about yourself
Disclosing information	Hiding or withholding information
Being open to new ideas or things that may be different from your own thinking	Dismissing others' ideas
Allowing others to see who you are	Creating layers that people cannot see through

2. Honest and with Integrity

This pair of qualities points to the mouth. Why? Because this is all about remembering to always be truthful and to watch what we say. Being honest and acting with integrity is all about telling the truth. But it's about telling the truth even when you might look bad or when the news is not that great. It is about behaving decently, fairly, and morally toward others. This meets others' needs for respect, fairness, and truth.

Someone who is not honest and lacks integrity might make up stories to look good, or that person might do something that is socially or culturally unacceptable and thus does not meet others' needs for respect, fairness, and truth.

See if you recognize the type of person in this example.

Barbara panicked as she watched her coffee splash onto her computer keyboard. Although she tried to mop it up, and she tipped the keyboard upside down and shook it, she knew she hadn't gotten it all. Soon thereafter, of course, the keys started sticking, and some of them didn't respond at all. To top it all off, the warranty on computer had just expired.

She took her laptop back to the store. "Listen, I don't know what happened. The keys just started sticking all of a sudden. I think you need to replace the laptop. I'm really not happy with it, and the screen has been acting up lately too," Barbara added, thinking that would add more authenticity to her story.

"Well, the warranty period is over, so we'll have to charge you to take a look to figure out what's wrong," said the store technician.

Honest and acting with integrity? Hmm.

But, you might be thinking, what could she have done, really? After all, she would have looked pretty dumb if she had told the truth, wouldn't she?

Here's a different scenario.

When Barbara spilled coffee on her keyboard, she rang the store and told them what happened. "I feel really stupid," she confessed.

"Hey, you wouldn't believe how many people do that!" consoles the technician. "The thing is, a lot of people try to cover it up. They must think *we're* stupid. We can tell they've dropped something on their computer. If you bring it down, we can lift the keyboard out for you and clean it right up."

Honest and acting with integrity? Yes, and it worked to Barbara's favor. Often our fear of looking silly can stop us from being honest. Sometimes it can appear that honesty will get us into trouble in some way, or we may not get what we want, but you know the saying: "Honesty is always the best policy!"

The chart that follows is a short summary of this pair of traits:

Honest and with Integrity	
Is	**Is Not**
Telling the truth	Lying
Telling the truth even if it's not great news	Telling 'half-truths' or stretching the truth to make things look better
Behaving decently and morally	Being disrespectful

3. Genuine and Authentic

This pair of qualities points to the heart. Why? Because this is all about remembering to always be true to ourselves, true to the core of who we are and what we stand for. Being genuine and authentic is the "what you see is what you get" quality. It's about behaving in a way that is consistent with who you are. It's being true to your core beliefs and values. Like being open and transparent, it provides others with more certainty about what they can expect from you.

Not being genuine and authentic is akin to wearing a costume. It's pretending to be something that you are not, often to please others.

Let's look at an example.

Andrea was going for a job interview. She really wanted the job, so she borrowed a suit from her sister to make sure she made a good impression.

At the interview they asked her if she was OK with occasionally working longer hours and traveling, as that would be required in the job.

"Oh, sure. I love traveling, and longer hours should be fine," Andrea said, but even as she answered she felt a bit sick. Her daughter was just three years old, and Andrea really wanted a job that allowed her more time at home, not less.

Genuine and authentic? Not really. Although Andrea does love traveling, and technically she was telling the truth, it really doesn't suit her at this time because it will clash with what is important to her—spending time with her daughter. Let's consider what else she could have said during the interview.

When the interviewer asked Andrea if she was available to work longer hours and to travel on business occasionally, she could have replied: "To be honest, I have a three-year-old. I love spending time with her, and I am concerned that if I am away from home too much, I'll worry about her and I won't perform my best for the company."

Genuine and authentic? Yes. You might be thinking, "Yes, but she won't get the job now, so that was dumb." I have a different view. I've done the whole "pretend to be someone you're not" thing, and it's really not sustainable. In the end, the real you wants to break out, and it does. Sometimes that can be a bit of a shock to those who thought you were something else. Andrea may not get this job, but when she lands a job that allows her to be true to herself, she will be much happier.

The chart that follows is a short summary of this pair of traits:

Genuine and Authentic	
Is	Is Not
This is me	'This is who I want you to think I am'
Behaving in a way that is consistent with who I am	Compromising on your values and beliefs
Being true	Being fake

4. Courageous and Decisive

This pair of qualities points to the stomach, or gut. Why? Because this is all about remembering to always have the courage to stand up for what is right, to make decisions even when it's tough. Being courageous and decisive means having the guts to stand up for what you believe in. It's about making a decision with conviction. It's going against what is "accepted" when what is accepted doesn't work anymore. This quality instills certainty, a sense of safety and security, which is a basic human need.

Someone who is not courageous and decisive procrastinates, makes decisions to suit whoever they are trying to please, and hides behind excuses.

See if you recognize the type in this example.

Jeff sat in the meeting and watched as the others on the executive team all nodded and agreed with the CEO. But he knew that if the company went down that track, they would get the same poor results they had got the previous year. Why wasn't anyone saying anything?

"You know what," Jeff piped up, "I think we have to take a different tack this time."

"What do you mean?" asked the CEO.

Jeff outlined his ideas and his reasons for doing something different. The CEO agreed, and then asked how the others felt about taking that approach.

"OK, I guess."

"Um, I think that might work."

"Well, I suppose we could give it a try."

Were the others in the executive team being courageous and decisive? Yes, but only once they knew it was reasonably safe to, and even then they were cautious. Jeff, on the other hand, was prepared to go against the flow, to put his point across, especially when he knew the original plan was likely to fail.

What stops people from being courageous and decisive? Fear: fear of looking silly, fear of the consequences of stepping out of line, or fear of losing their job. I can tell you now, though, that the most valuable employees are the ones who challenge the norms when there is a better way: It is from this that you get true innovation.

The chart that follows is a short summary of this pair of traits:

Courageous and Decisive	
Is	Is Not
Having the guts to stand up for what is right	Sitting back while the wrong things get repeated
Making a decision with conviction	Making decisions only to please others, or procrastinating
Going against the norms when the norms don't work or there is a better way	Unnecessary risk taking

5. Reliable and Proven

This pair of qualities points to the legs. Why? Because this is all about remembering to always walk the talk. Being reliable and proven is all about doing what you say you are going to do and consistently delivering on promises. It's being dependable. This meets others' expectations and needs, and it is all about keeping the promises you've made.

Someone who is not reliable and proven says one thing and does another, lets people down, and overpromises and underdelivers. (This has been a real issue for me personally, and something I have had to face up to in order to maintain my own credibility, given what I talk about!)

Let's look at an example in real life.

Brett was talking to Carl, the manufacturing manager at one of Brett's biggest customers. "Yeah, sure, Carl, I can have the materials to you on Monday."

"Are you sure, Brett? We have a backlog here and really need those materials. The orders keep coming in and we're getting hammered by the retailers," said Carl somewhat anxiously.

"Hey, come on, I said Monday, didn't I? I'll get my boys on it right away for you."

Monday morning came and went. By Monday afternoon Carl was beside himself. He rang Brett.

"Oh, listen, Carl, we had a bit of a problem with some of our other deliveries, but we'll have the materials you ordered there tomorrow. You have my word."

Reliable and proven? Brett has just broken the wall of trust. We all know people like this. It can be very easy to make a promise and then expect others to understand when we can't deliver. What could Brett have done differently?

This time when Brett talks to Carl, he could be honest and say something like, "I think I can get you the materials on Monday, but I have to tell you we have a lot of other deliveries to make at the moment."

When Carl explains, anxiously, all the pressure he's under to fulfill the manufacturing plant's orders, Brett could then respond with a compromise such as: "I can probably get you half the materials by Monday, and I'll bring it by myself on my way through. But, realistically, the other half won't get to you 'til Tuesday. Does that help?"

On Monday after lunch, Brett delivers half the order, and as promised, has the other half delivered on Tuesday. Carl was able to let his manufacturing people know in advance so they could manage their workflow to suit.

Reliable and proven? Yes. Being reliable and proven is really all about thinking, "Can I actually do what it is I am committing to in the time frame I have promised?" It means taking the time to think something through so you don't end up constantly breaking promises. It often means managing people's expectations by letting them know what is possible, thus saving bricks in both the promises wall and the expectations wall.

The chart that follows is a short summary of this pair of traits:

Reliable and Proven	
Is	**Is Not**
Doing what I say I'll do	Saying one thing and doing another
Consistently delivering	Delivering some of the time
Managing expectations and meeting needs	Building up expectations and letting people down

6. Caring and Empathetic

This pair of qualities points to the feet or shoes. Why? Because this is all about remembering to always put yourself in the other person's shoes, to consider their point of view. Being caring and empathetic is about thinking about where others might be coming from and ultimately doing things that benefit them. This is about taking the time to find out what others expect and need from you and actively finding ways to meet—or manage—those expectations and needs. It is also recognizing that respect is a human need.

Someone who is not caring and empathetic is out for her- or himself alone, behaves in ways that impact negatively on others, and is oblivious, selfish, or uncaring.

Here's a true-to-life example.

Brianna was so excited. As soon as she heard the news that she had been chosen to lead the project, she couldn't wait to go and tell her colleagues.

Aaron was disappointed when he heard the news. He himself had been waiting for an opportunity like that for a while. He had even told his manager he would love to lead the project and would take time to train someone to fill in for him at his job until he was able to come back. Brianna knew that Aaron had applied for the project leadership position.

"Hey, Brianna. Congratulations on getting the project manager role. Listen, did they say anything about the selection process?" Aaron asked.

"Not really. The quality of the other applicants made the decision easy for them, I guess," she said with a smile as she turned to talk to another coworker.

Caring and empathetic? No, but we've all seen this kind of behavior, and may very well have participated in it ourselves at some stage. Whether Brianna was deliberately being catty or was just insensitive we really don't know, but the important thing to recognize is that in such situations, such a response can be perceived as being uncaring.

How could this scene play out differently?

This time when Aaron asks her whether the managers said anything about the selection process, Brianna could reply: "Not to me. I'm sorry you missed out, Aaron. I know you were eager to lead this project. Maybe if you talk to your manager he might be able to give you an idea of what they were specifically looking for. If you'd like, I could recommend you as a backup," she added.

Caring and empathetic? Yes. Brianna was considerate of how Aaron might be feeling and behaved in a way that was sensitive to that. As we all know, there are disappointments in life, and we don't always get what we want. But we do want to be treated with respect and fairness, and we will trust those who are able to master this.

The chart that follows is a short summary of this pair of traits:

Caring and Empathetic	
Is	**Is Not**
Considering others	Being selfish
Understanding the expectations and needs of others	Brushing people off
Putting yourself in others' shoes	Only looking after your own interests

ARE YOU TRUSTWORTHY?

Now that you've learned about the qualities of a trustworthy person, it's time to test yourself. Here are some questions for you to answer to determine how trustworthy you are.

Do this quick assessment and check your score at the end. Rate each question on the scale of 1 to 5:

1 = almost never

2 = rarely

3 = sometimes

4 = frequently

5 = almost always

Then tally your score.

Be honest. The only person you will be kidding is yourself if you are not truthful.

Openness and Transparency	
When someone tells me something I don't agree with, I still listen and think about it	1 2 3 4 5
I let people know if I am having a bad day or something is bothering me	1 2 3 4 5
I share information about something I know about, unless I have promised not to	1 2 3 4 5
Score (Total of all questions)	

Honesty and with Integrity	
I tell the truth, even if it might make me look bad	1 2 3 4 5
I treat people fairly	1 2 3 4 5
I behave ethically	1 2 3 4 5
Score (Total of all questions)	

Genuine and Authentic	
What you see is what you get with me	1 2 3 4 5
I am clear in my own mind about what is important to me	1 2 3 4 5
My own values and the company's values are aligned	1 2 3 4 5
Score (Total of all questions)	

Courageous and Decisive	
When I make a decision, I am clear it is the right thing	1 2 3 4 5
I stand up for what I believe is right, even if others might criticize me	1 2 3 4 5
I admit when I've made a mistake	1 2 3 4 5
Score (Total of all questions)	

Reliable and Proven	
If I promise it, I deliver it	1 2 3 4 5
I am consistent in what I do	1 2 3 4 5
I can be depended upon	1 2 3 4 5
Score (Total of all questions)	

Caring and Empathetic	
I take time to understand the expectations and needs of others	1 2 3 4 5
I consider how other people might be feeling	1 2 3 4 5
I sit quietly and listen when someone is talking to me	1 2 3 4 5
Score (Total of all questions)	
Overall Score	

How did you do? Was there one area that stood out as much higher than the others? Was there an area that stood out as much lower than the others?

If you scored:

72–90: You are doing great, and have people who trust you and depend on you. Well done.

54–71: You are on the way to developing your trustworthiness. Take a look at the areas you scored lower on and think about what you can do differently to improve.

36–53: You may notice that you are often in conflict with others, or there may be tension in your relationships. Start working today to improve those areas where you scored the lowest!

18–35: You may want a coach or a mentor to help you work on the areas where you have scored the lowest. Your ability to build and maintain healthy relationships at work really depends on you improving your trustworthiness.

If you would like some support in building your own trustworthiness, visit www.entente.com.au and ask us about coaching and mentoring.

GETTING THE BALANCE RIGHT

Now that we've looked at the six qualities of a trustworthy person, and you've answered the questions about your own level of trustworthiness, what is really important to understand is that the qualities must work together; they must be balanced.

Just like our body needs to be in balance to function well, so our trustworthy qualities need to be balanced in order for people to rely on us to deliver the outcomes they want.

If these qualities get out of balance, with high scores in some areas and low scores in others, the outcomes could be… well, let's look at some examples.

High	Low	Outcome
Open and transparent	Courageous and decisive	Very open to new ideas and sharing of self, but could be getting confused with information and then procrastinating – not meeting expectations or keeping promises
Honest and with Integrity	Caring and Empathetic	May think you are doing the right thing telling people the truth, but could be coming across as insensitive – not meeting basic needs

High	Low	Outcome
Genuine and Authentic	Reliable and Proven	Very comfortable with who you are, really nice person, but not delivering on anything you are promising
Courageous and Decisive	Open and Transparent	Very good at making decisions, but not sharing them with anyone or explaining your reasons – not meeting basic needs
Reliable and Proven	Honest and with Integrity	Very good at getting things done, but just not necessarily the right things – not meeting expectations or needs
Caring and Empathetic	Genuine and Authentic	Very good at putting yourself out for others, but compromising your values, eventually getting annoyed and backing off – not keeping promises

So, you can see how important it is that we work to maintain a healthy balance in order to be consistently trustworthy. And because trust is such a precious gift, it's worth the effort!

Now let's read what our experts have to say about the importance of trustworthiness in all aspects of business life.

Something to Do

How high was your trustworthiness score? Write down on a piece of paper what you are now going to do differently to improve your level of trustworthiness. Keep it with you as a reminder—in your wallet, on your desk, on your refrigerator, wherever you will see it on a regular basis—and make the change!

13

TRUST IN LEADERSHIP

Trust is the essence of Leadership.
—Colin Powell, former Secretary of State,
United States of America

INTRODUCING MANDY HOLLOWAY

A mutual friend introduced me to Mandy, and she instantly struck me as a genuine and authentic person. She has a business that focuses on connecting existing leaders with emerging leaders. By giving these leaders the confidence to have courageous conversations, she supports them securing the brand, people, and financial sustainability of their organization. Mandy does this by providing:

- Leadership development programs
- "Leading Change" workshops
- High-performance culture-development programs
- Executive coaching programs

- Career mentoring services
- Keynote speaking
- Facilitation services

Understanding the ongoing pressures faced by business leaders comes naturally to Mandy through her personal leadership experiences as a partner of KPMG (a global company offering audit, tax, and advisory services) and, more recently, the challenging experiences with her diverse client base. Combining her strong business background with her learning expertise means she designs, develops, and delivers learning solutions that achieve sustainable results for her clients. (For more details about her company, go to www.hollowayconsulting.com.au.)

Some of her recent projects include leadership development programs for Tower; development and delivery of PricewaterhouseCoopers Summit program, supporting the final career progression for future partners; redesigning the Public Practice Program for the Institute of Chartered Accountants in Australia, with self- directed and experiential learning components; and mentoring the careers of many women in senior leadership positions in business.

PUTTING IT INTO PERSPECTIVE

It is the leaders in an organization who drive the purpose and ignite the passion to build and create the organization's sustainability—its financial, people, and brand sustainability. This kind of sustainability builds when you have total alignment with the financial, people, and brand goals.

I have worked with leadership and management teams over the last fifteen years and am constantly amazed at this lack of alignment. Just recently I sat in the foyer of a global business and watched in awe as an amazing message came on the huge plasma screen attached to the wall. The message left me inspired and excited about what this business stood for. So, you can imagine the shock I felt when the person I was visiting—who was employed as a senior executive in the business—feigned ignorance about the message as we rode in the elevator and dismissed it as another one of those marketing gimmicks that everyone forgets to tell us about!!

I wonder how much money they spent on the marketing campaign. Leaders need to set out the expectations and ensure that everyone's needs are taken into account within the promises they make. Leadership builds trust within the internal and external stakeholders of an organization every day.

To build this kind of sustainability, to get it right, to create this infectious commitment many organizations are investing substantially in time, money, and emotions to identify their core operating values and build the culture so they "live" these values every day. They are beginning to see these values and the culture as the foundation of financial, people, and brand sustainability in their organization.

Conceptually, many leaders are beginning to understand that it is these values that determine the behaviors everyone needs to commit to in order to build the culture that makes the organization

- attract customers
- generate revenue/sales and produce a strong bottom line
- an attractive place to work and belong
- a highly respected and trusted brand
- add value to the national and global economy

PEOPLE SUSTAINABILITY IS CRITICAL

As we enter times of great change in the labor market, people sustainability increases in its criticality to business leaders. At the heart of people sustainability is the perception that people have about the "way they need to work to be recognized, rewarded, and to ultimately fit in with the organization." Get this right, make the organization attractive to people, have people connected to the purpose and passion espoused by the leaders—then you build people sustainability.

Why, then, are many organizations still failing to succeed with people sustainability? Many continue to incur high staff turnover rates, lower productivity rates than they would like, low engagement levels with their people, and many other measurable symptoms. The answer is generally quite simple: This failure is largely attributed to the top leadership group who are failing to recognize the importance of matching their own behavior to these values and the expectations set when espousing what the organization should look like.

Herein rests a critical foundation of trust in leadership. People within the organization want to see actions matching words; then and only then can they have trust in leadership.

What About People Outside the Organization?

Today there are more stakeholders to trust in leadership than the people within the organization: There are customers/clients, shareholders, potential investors, the Board of Directors, lenders of debt finance (like banks,) and they all need trust in leadership too.

The trust they look for is linked to each of financial, people, and brand sustainability. These stakeholders look to business leaders to successfully manage this ongoing tension within the business. This tension permeates every decision they make, each behavior they choose, and every promise they make.

BUILDING TRUST IN YOUR LEADERSHIP MASTERY

Leaders are not born; there is not a leadership gene that only some people inherit! Leaders need to develop their mastery, and they need to do it in such a way that they maximize their natural strengths and beliefs while minimizing the impact of their "leadership demons."

I have worked with an incredible variety of people all striving to develop their leadership mastery. Not only do they need to develop skills, tactics, and passion so key stakeholders want to believe in them and want to follow them; they also need to create the personal vision, to find the passion, and to build skills so they can believe in themselves.

Having designed many leadership development programs, I rely on my framework for leadership mastery—a framework that is easily understood and easily applied to any kind of business.

To lead an organization and its people with purpose and passion, I believe leaders need leadership mastery spanning four critical areas:

- Self-mastery
- Business mastery
- Relationship mastery
- Technical mastery

The following table overlays leadership mastery with elements of trust and trustworthiness.

Mastery	Self	Business	Relationship	Technical
Need this mastery so you can develop:	Authentic Courageous Passionate Congruent **Personal success**	Insightful Practical Resourceful Decisive **Financial success**	Trusted by people who work with you – Engaging Inspiring **Professional success**	Intellectually stimulating Competent Ethical **Strong professional reputation**
Want to build trust with the key stakeholder groups of:	Self	Staff Peers The Board Shareholders Business analysts Lenders Customers Suppliers	Staff Peers Customers Suppliers Alliance partners Your boss	Staff Customers Peers Your boss
These key stakeholders groups expect that:	You can be the kind of leader you want to be	You make the right decisions for the future sustainability of the business	What you say is what you do – you are a person who delivers!	You develop the products, services and solutions that deliver value
A trustworthy person in leadership is perceived as fulfilling the criteria of:	Genuine and Authentic Honesty and Integrity	Reliable and Proven Honesty and Integrity	Openness and Transparency Selfless and Empathetic Genuine and Authentic	Reliable and Proven

As you can see from this table, trust is at the heart of each facet of leadership mastery. Let's explore each of these facets in more detail.

1. Self-Mastery

Self-mastery is all about you having the confidence to be the kind of leader you want to be—becoming your "ideal self" as a leader. In this way you achieve personal success because you are

- Authentic
- Courageous
- Passionate
- Congruent

For leaders to be all of these, they need to "trust themselves" to behave in a way that consistently fits with their personal values and their view of ideal self as a leader. To do this you need to do the thinking and engage the heart!

Do the Thinking What does ideal self as a leader look like?

How can others have trust in your leadership if you do not! You need to like what you stand for as a leader and as a person who fills many roles in life: spouse, parent, child, sister/brother, business leader, community member, member of a sports team, and so on.

Others expect to see you confidently developing into the kind of leader you are proud to be—not apologizing for things you have missed or expressing feelings of guilt or trying to be perfect and show that you have all of the answers all of the time. You need to show others that you are real. They want you to be authentic. They want you to be courageous and admit when you make mistakes, and they want you to be honest and act with integrity by admitting your weaknesses.

Gordon Cairns, former CEO at Lion Nathan and previously voted a Financial Times BOSS True Leader, said at a CEO Forum Group in December 2004: "You can only develop if you are getting feedback. Having got that feedback, you then need to do something useful with it."

According to Rob Goffee of the London Business School, "There is nothing more annoying and less likely to establish trust and loyalty than the perfect boss—the one whose hair is always in place, who is never rattled by situations, the one who is bright and perky at 8:30 AM on a Monday morning" (excerpted from *Why Should Anyone Be Led by You? What It Takes to Be an Authentic Leader*, Harvard Business School Press, 2006).

How often have you heard your leaders own up to their mistakes and their foibles? How often have you done it with your employees while undertaking a leadership role?

Coaching many young businesspeople as they prepare for the transition into business leadership, I ask them, "What does your 'ideal self as a leader' look like?" Most of them will not have a ready answer and will need time to think about it, and I generally need to tease their ideas out and really challenge their thinking. It is this type of thinking that builds trust in self as a potential business leader who can create success for all key stakeholders, including themselves! Many need to go on a journey to discover and identify their values.

Engage the Heart—Know Your Values and Live Your Values To be passionate, have congruence, and be authentic, you need to engage your heart—by knowing your values and living them every day. I start this journey with people as they embark on leadership development programs. For many it is the first time they have really sat and thought about it, and very much the first time they have had to write them down and think about how they live them every day! When someone asks me if I mean career values or work values, then I know immediately that they are in the "achieve" act of life.

Let me explain. If you are one of those people who need to ask if I am referring to personal or career values, this is an indication of which "act in life" you are currently playing. In their book *Managing by Values: How to Put Your Values into Action for Extraordinary Results* (Berrett-Koehler Publishers, 2nd edition, 2003), Ken Blanchard and Michael O'Connor describe the three acts in life as they see them:

1. Achieve

2. Connect

3. Integrate

If you are in the "achieve" act of life, then you are striving for certain goals and are prepared to forgo some of your values in the workplace so that you can achieve them! When reading Blanchard's book for the first time, I could absolutely relate to this because during the first ten years of my career, I wanted to achieve my goal of being a partner in a professional service firm, and I can now recognize that I did not live all of my values in the workplace. For example, I lived my value of freedom outside of the workplace by rappelling, camping in the wilderness, and sailing; it was not possible for me to exercise freedom in the workplace as a junior person wanting to get recognized enough to progress within the hierarchy of the business.

"Connect" is about relationships—being with people who are important to you and you can connect with at a level relevant and appropriate for you. I know that once I had "achieved" my goal and had become a partner in the firm, I began to focus more on the kind of relationships I was developing. I looked around to ensure that I was building the kind of relationships where I was really connecting with people: my clients, my staff, and especially my fellow partners. I needed to feel "in" on things and included.

Many people do not ever arrive at the "integrate" act because they are very happy with either of the first two acts. Integrate is about bringing the first two acts together and really living your life completely true to your values every day and in every way! I can recall one day sitting in my office as a partner in a very successful firm thinking this was not what I wanted. I was finding it increasingly difficult to live my values every day and in every way that was congruent with both the values of the firm and my fellow partners while still connecting at a relationship level with them. So I moved out into my own consulting business so I could live in the act of integrate.

Some people choose to stay in the first act for their entire life and are happy and fulfilled to do so while others, like me, will find it imperative for happiness, passion, and authenticity to move to the third act.

Whatever the act of life you choose to operate in, it is critical that as a leader you know your values and live your values! It is only when you are doing this that you can "trust" yourself to behave in a way that consistently fits with your personal values and your view of ideal self as a leader. It is only then that you can confidently know what you need as a leader and can then set realistic and authentic expectations that culminate in promises you know you can keep!

2. Business Mastery

At the heart of the financial sustainability of an organization is the capability of its leaders to make sound business decisions. Key stakeholders want to develop trust in this leadership to make the "right" decisions. They want the leadership to show they are insightful, practical, resourceful, and, lastly, decisive. Financial success is paramount: it is measured and reported to key stakeholders.

To develop trust that the leadership decisions will be right, these key stakeholders need to see and feel congruence with the values of the organization and the values of the person in the leadership role. People know what to expect because of the espoused and published organizational values, the brand promise, the financial forecasts made public, and the interactions with people in the organization. For trust in their business mastery, key stakeholders need to see actions matching these promises and matching the personal values of the leader.

What, then, are the key issues we need to consider when building trust in our business mastery? In building such mastery we need to see

- Congruence with values, personal and organizational
- Evidence of an ethical and "trusted" business conscience
- Propensity to trust and how it impacts the way leaders do business
- Communication of decisions to key stakeholders

Congruence with Values Values are intrinsic when making any business decision—to the person in the leadership role and to the organization, its brand promise, and its culture. This is where self-mastery and business mastery intersect for the individual and where others will feel and see the congruence and authenticity.

It is important for leaders to know and understand and personally connect with the values of the organization. The people that come to work for that organization, the customers that buy from it, the suppliers, the shareholders, every stakeholder is relying on the leaders of the organization to live, every day, by the values. If this cannot be done, then the values should not be stated in the first place. You cannot on one hand say, "This is who we are," then on the other hand behave in a way that is totally incongruent with your values.

Too many organizations have the mission, vision, and values plastered on walls, mouse pads, and Web sites, but their behaviors do not match them. Worse still, there are often no consequences for incongruent behavior—that is, except for a breakdown of trust!

Being in congruence with the organization's values and being able to make decisions based on those values is incredibly powerful, empowering, and imperative to building trust with others.

Evidence of a "Trusted" Business Conscience Key stakeholders need to know that the leaders of any organization can be trusted for their ethical behavior and decisions. They need to be able to trust their business conscience, and that they will "do the right thing."

Brad Goldschmidt, Joint Managing Director of InsuranceLine, in his August 2005 interview with Vanessa Hall about trust, talked about the increasing number of contracts and legislation in business. As he says, the contract becomes the "conscience. Legislation proves that the regulators don't trust the industry or businesses operating in it."

I absolutely concur with this interesting and very sad insight. I have personally experienced far too many examples of trust in business conscience being replaced by contracts and more legislation. These written documents are there to either close down the loopholes many business leaders find and exploit, or fight the deceit and poor ethical behavior of business leaders.

From the surveys and interviews Vanessa Hall and Entente have conducted over the past few years, the words most commonly associated with people you trust least in your life are, among others, deceitful, game playing, selfish, arrogant, cold, inconsistent, superficial, self-interested, disrespectful, façade, and lying to try and gain an advantage.

When these words are associated with people we encounter who are leading businesses, we have a serious problem. Until leaders can be trusted to make ethical business decisions, there will be a continued cost to doing business by having to dot every "I" and cross every "T" in legal contracts that attempt to force a trusted consciousness.

What happened to the old-fashioned symbol of trust—the handshake? Instead of a handshake we now need handcuffs in the form of a contract to force companies to do the right thing!

A trusted business conscience requires leadership mastery that considers the overall business strategy; the purpose, mission and values of the organization; and the promises that have been made to all stakeholders, plus being able to balance decision making for the future sustainability of the business. That is what is needed, that is what is expected of leaders, and that is what those who take the seat at the head of the table have promised.

Propensity to Trust Is there an innate propensity to trust? Do some people trust more than others? Is it something we learn?

In my experience there are definitely people who seem to trust more than others, and I have certainly come across some senior people who do not trust anyone at all! Some people may find, like me, that they have a high propensity to trust. Then there are others who are very cynical and dubious about trusting anyone else, especially in senior roles within an organization. Rohan Gamble, previous managing director of Virgin Money Australia, stated in an interview Vanessa Hall had with him in July 2005 that "Unfortunately, I've found that the more senior my roles have become, the more exposed I become to untrusting people, and I think that's sad."

Bad experiences and a driving need to protect ourselves as we move up the organizational hierarchy and to protect the organization have driven our business leaders to have a low propensity to trust. If this continues, then key stakeholders will continue to have low trust in the leaders' business mastery, and business leaders will be locked into a situation where they feel they need to somehow maintain control in order to ensure the business outcomes they are driving.

Innovation and change require trust. In a business world where competition is rife, where your next year's competitor does not even exist yet, leaders need to build a trusting business environment where they can lead innovative thinking, keep up with the pace of change, and reinvent the organization to meet the growing needs and expectations of consumers.

A survey by PriceWaterhouseCoopers in 2000 of three hundred large companies found that the existence of high trust levels was crucial for successful innovation. If leaders are bound up with a low propensity to trust—that is, they have difficulty relying on others to produce the outcomes needed—they stifle innovation in their own organizations.

Changing this situation is vital to the future sustainability of organizations. It is reassuring to know that research overwhelmingly supports that some people are developing a greater propensity to trust: personality traits, habits built as a child, learned at school. And the research of American psychologist Martin Seligman reassures us further that people *can* learn to be optimistic, they *can* learn to trust in the goodness of others.

Tests are available to check on your propensity to trust; they provide tangible evidence of something you need to know as a business leader. The trust radius test developed by Q Metrics is one such test. I took it, and the conclusion came back that I expected other people to be trustworthy, to treat me fairly, and to be inherently "good." This confirmed something I had intuitively known for years, but it gave me concrete evidence that I could now use and further develop. (For more about this test visit www.essisystems.com.)

The test also went on to conclude that those who show strong capacities on this scale are able *to use trust in a transformational way.* Their belief system frees them to suspend judgment. Couple this with the understanding of what trust is and how to build it in business, and we have the recipe for transformational leadership.

Thankfully, I can proudly state that while facilitating leadership development programs I can count on one hand the number of times people have broken my trust. So, there has to be something to inherently trusting people until they do something to break your trust!

Communicating Decisions The final section in building trust in your business mastery has to be in your ability, capability, and courage to communicate your decisions very openly and very honestly, without holding back information. Unfortunately, there is the "keep them in the dark" syndrome that is alive and well throughout business.

Decisions are often made without consultation and then without sufficient communication and buy-in. This is a major contributing factor to a lack of trust many key stakeholders have in the business mastery of leaders. Our initial reaction is to question the ethics, integrity, or correctness of a decision when it is finally communicated or leaked through the organization.

Poor communication creates an instant fear: "What is really going on?" "Is my job under threat?" "Why haven't we been told?" People generally prefer bad news to no news. Not communicating decisions or not involving people in the solutions to business issues just leaves people guessing, and often the picture they create in their own minds is worse than the reality.

Communicating decisions involves a strong element of vulnerability, and this is where many business leaders opt out, because it is easier and safer to keep the knowledge to themselves. They choose actions such as these instead:

- To "leak" the decision over time
- To share it in a quiet and less overt way
- To make a brash and commanding statement that has the undertone of "don't question me or my decision"
- To let people find out for themselves as they experience the impact of the decision (like a new policy or system)

I think we need to break down people's fear of being courageous, of being vulnerable and really exposing what they think and feel.

External and internal stakeholders want the business leadership to be open and transparent, reliable and proven. They want to know the decisions that will be made can be relied on and are trustworthy. They need to know that the leadership act with integrity and will always be honest; then they know they have trust in the business mastery of their leadership!

3. Relationship Mastery

Relationship mastery is all about others knowing that what you say is what you will do. Others can include such stakeholders as your staff, customers/clients, suppliers, the business owners, and alliance business partners. This is where it is vital for you to "walk in the shoes" of the other person. Relationship mastery is only as successful as your capability to communicate openly and honestly with other people. This is totally dependent on the trust you have built within the relationships you have with these other people.

What, then, are the key issues we need to consider when building trust in our relationship mastery? In building such mastery we need to

- Think the best not the worst, to suspend judgment
- Listen with the intent to understand
- Have the courage to share
- Take responsibility for our actions and the perceptions they create

Think the Best, Not the Worst I always say to those people I live with, work with, play with, "Think the best of me when you are in doubt about my intentions." It is then up to me to work incredibly hard to build a level of trust where people feel they are able to do this.

I find it very sad that so many people have a natural propensity to jump in and think the worst of you: They see your behavior and hear your words and jump to the "bad" conclusion, often without even talking it through with you. I am prompted to recall this story that Stephen Covey tells in his book *The 7 Habits of Highly Effective People* (Free Press, 15th anv. ed., 2004) about such an event that happened to him. After reading this story I have certainly challenged myself to suspend judgment and engage in open discussion to explore the intention behind another person's words or behavior.

I remember a mini-paradigm shift I experienced one Sunday morning on a subway in New York. People were sitting quietly—some reading newspapers, some lost in thought, some resting with their eyes closed. It was a calm, peaceful scene.

Then suddenly, a man and his children entered the subway car. The children were so loud and rambunctious that instantly the whole climate changed.

The man sat down next to me and closed his eyes, apparently oblivious to the situation. The children were yelling back and forth, throwing things, even grabbing people's papers. It was very disturbing. And yet, the man sitting next to me did nothing.

It was difficult not to feel irritated. I could not believe that he could be so insensitive as to let his children run wild like that and do nothing about it, taking no responsibility at all. It was easy to see that everyone else on the subway felt irritated too. So finally, with what I felt was unusual patience and restraint, I turned to him and said, "Sir, your children are really disturbing a lot of people. I wonder if you couldn't control them a little more."

The man lifted his gaze as if to come to a consciousness of the situation for the first time and said softly, "Oh, you're right. I guess I should do something about it. We just came from the hospital where their mother died about an hour ago. I don't know what to think, and I guess they don't know how to handle it either."

Can you imagine what I felt at that moment? My paradigm shifted. Suddenly I saw things differently, and because I saw differently, I thought differently, I felt differently, I behaved differently.

Listen with the Intent to Understand A critical element of building trust in your relationship mastery is the ability to listen: to listen with the intent to understand and not with the intent to respond. In my experience, people in positions of leadership who really do this well are quite rare. I have experienced far too many people in leadership roles sitting, "listening" but what they are really doing is taking the time out while the other person is talking, preparing themselves to

- Defend their actions or those of others
- Justify why they took the actions or chose the behavior
- Blame someone else or something else for the actions that were taken or the behavior that they chose

- Deceive or manipulate the person
- Protect themselves from further "attack"

Listening, true listening, involves clearing the mind, suspending judgment, and being completely open to what the other person has to say. It demonstrates respect for the other person, a basic need we have as human beings.

Have the Courage to Share The inverse element of listening is the ability and courage to share or expose your ideas, thoughts, and feelings. By using both these elements you create an "open window" for your relationship where trust is deep and can be relied upon when the parties are interacting. A widely used framework to describe the inverse nature of these elements is the Johari Window, shown here.

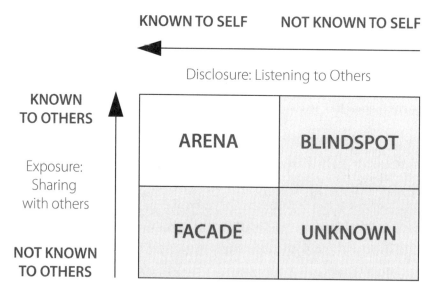

The Johari Window: A graphic model of interpersonal awareness

Source: J. Luft and H. Ingham, Proceedings of the Western Training Laboratory in Group Development (Los Angeles: UCLA Press, 1955)

By sharing your innermost thoughts and ideas (in the "open" section of the window), you make yourself vulnerable, and this is why many business leaders refrain from doing this. Consequently, they can cut themselves off from developing enriched and productive relationships with people and with key stakeholders. They choose to operate with a "façade," and over time this gets bigger and in the way of developing real relationships.

In my experience it is at about this time that business leaders lose their soul, their passion for what they do, because they have lost touch with their values as a person. Their defense mechanisms are well and truly honed, and they let no one into the core of who they really are and how they really feel. People develop greater trust for leaders who are "real," who they can have some kind of relationship with, and who they know are, in many ways, just like them.

Take Responsibility for Our Actions and the Perceptions They Create In my experience, this element is critical to healthy relationships where others can trust that what you say is what you will do. You are engaging and inspiring because you take full responsibility for your actions and the perceptions they create. Again, this is something that is difficult to do because it is so much easier as a leader, a person with positional power, to blame others or to justify your behavior. It is far more difficult to actually take full responsibility!

Try it tomorrow: For a whole day you are not allowed to blame anyone or anything for errors or things that go wrong; you need to take personal responsibility for the fact it did not work!

I recall a rather tough assignment in which I was being considered as a consultant for a very senior partner in an accounting firm. I worked very hard to drop my ego and use a highly facilitative style, never taking ownership for ideas produced as we worked together across the table. I also worked very hard not to match any of his aggressive behavior, responding instead with encouraging and supportive behavior. When I was dismissed from the assignment rather than being hired, I was told that the senior partner had decided he did not want to work with me because he did not think I was adding any value. I wanted to scream out and blame him. After all, he had "stolen my ideas," he had talked over the top of me, and he had avoided my requests for clarity on what he wanted and expected from me.

It was really hard for me to take responsibility for having created his perceptions and then living with the consequences of that.

We've all heard the saying "perception is reality," and as a leader, your stakeholders will have all kinds of perceptions of who you are; your actions, your behavior will drive many of those perceptions. Blaming others is pretty useless. Take responsibility and change the way you do things. Build trust by creating new, more meaningful expectations of who you are as a leader.

A SPECIAL LEARNING POINT

While reflecting on some of my personal experiences in preparation for writing this chapter, I recalled feedback that I had received on several occasions. At first this feedback had confused me. Several senior people within the business in which I was a senior executive had told me I was naive. Through much soul searching I was able to create clarity for myself, and it was a wonderful insight for my self-mastery, business mastery, and relationship mastery! People were confusing my propensity to trust others and think the best of them with naïveté. They were so very wrong.

They assumed that because I did not retaliate, defend, or justify I was naive. They felt that because I trusted people right away without "testing them," without playing games, and without making life a little difficult for them and expecting them to do the wrong thing I was naïve, and even "gullible." They found it impossible to believe that when I knew what other people were up to and chose not to retaliate, not to play the game, I could actually be doing this in an intellectually and emotionally informed way! By choosing this kind of strategy I had made myself very vulnerable in relationship mastery and yet totally empowered in self-mastery. Would I do it again? Absolutely!

Relationship mastery in leaders is all about vulnerability and courage. Leaders need to stand tall and be honest; they need to take responsibility for their actions and stop blaming. They really need to think the best of others.

4. Technical Mastery

When you have technical mastery, you have both guru status and a strong professional reputation. Technical mastery is all about others knowing that you develop products, services, and solutions that deliver value and fall within the defined legislative constraints—like tax legislation, for example.

This facet of leadership mastery is one that is emphasized throughout the career of a business leader and yet has the least impact on trust in leadership itself. Why, you might ask? Think about an engineer, an accountant, an architect, a lawyer; they spend their study/qualifying time developing their technical mastery. They use their skills to advance their career. Then it is their guru status that gains them their right to become a business leader. They were trusted because they could be relied upon to produce an outcome that was needed—that is, to build a reliable and aesthetically pleasing building, or to produce a set of reliable and correct accounts, for example.

Leadership, being at the forefront of a business, a project, or a team has very little to do with your technical mastery, and everything to do with who you are, how you behave, and how you engage and motivate those you need to have follow you on your mission.

It is for this reason that we have spent more time focusing on self-mastery, business mastery, and relationship mastery. One of the biggest mistakes organizations make is promoting technically competent people into leadership roles. This can create distrust all around.

1. The promoted staff themselves begin to lose trust in their own capability. They used to be loved and rewarded for their work, and now they can't seem to get a group of people to follow them. Their self-trust can break down.
2. Those responsible for the promotions lose trust in those they've promoted. They used to be good at what they did, but now they can't make a business decision to save their life. The trust the shareholders or directors had in the senior leaders can break down.

3. Those expected to follow the newly promoted leaders lose trust in them. They might have been good at what they did, but they haven't got a clue about how to build relationships with people. The trust their followers had in them breaks down.

Key stakeholders learn to "respect" the business leader because they have strong technical mastery; they can trust the solution and the advice, but they do not have trust with the business leader as a person.

This is where business and relationship mastery are essential and far more important to the issue of trust in leadership.

I'd like to focus on a couple of excellent points Mandy made in this chapter, drawing on the trust model and the attributes of the trustworthy person listed earlier.

VALUES ALIGNMENT AND TRUST

Mandy talked about the importance of leaders living the values of the organization, walking the talk, and the expectations that people have that the espoused values are demonstrated in the organization.

Let's take a look at a hypothetical example.

Trustus, an up and coming company, had prominently set out these three values on their Web site:

- Integrity
- Respect
- Caring

Angela read this as she was preparing for her job interview with Trustus. It made her feel comfortable that she was doing the right thing; the company values really aligned with hers.

Here's Angela's ENP wall at this point:

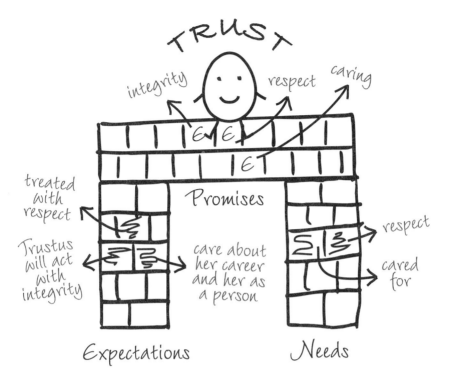

Angela was hired, and in a meeting with her manager and two of the executives a few months later, she raised an issue she had discovered. One of the executives interrupted her dismissively, and her manager glared at her and shook his head.

After the meeting, her manager called Angela into his office. "What do you think you're doing?"

"Well, what you were talking about will have a significant impact on the product development plans. It could impact the customers negatively. I thought it was worth discussing," she said, quite confident of her position.

"Look. I don't need you prancing around making me look bad. You were brought here because we need that product out on the market. Can you do that or can't you? Because if you can't, then maybe you're not the right person for the job."

What happened to Angela's ENP wall from a values perspective?

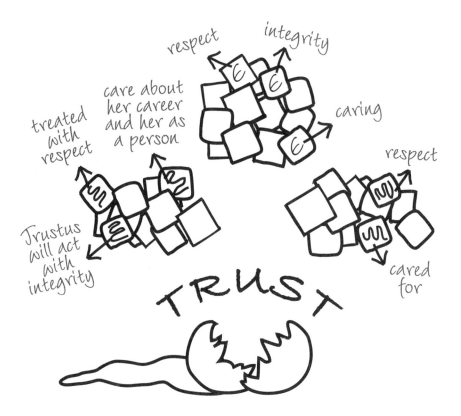

There is very little value alignment. Executives are behaving in ways that are inconsistent with the company's espoused values.

Is this an extreme example? Frankly, I've seen worse, and I've been personally exposed to worse. Mandy has clearly seen this sort of thing a number of times in her work. As she has said, leaders need to be living and breathing the values; if not, they are breaking down trust on a daily basis in their own organizations.

LISTENING AND TRUST

Mandy spoke about the importance of listening with an intent to understand the other person. Is this a lost art? Are we even taught to properly listen?

I remember I had a manager who would repeatedly tell us, "My door is always open." He would ask us to come and talk to him if we had any problems. "Great," I thought. I was trying to get a bunch of people to understand the importance of compliance and was facing some resistance. Maybe my manager would have some views on how to better handle the situation.

I knocked on his door. "Have you got a few minutes? I've got a problem," I said as I stuck my head around the door to his office.

"Sure, come in. Sit down." I sat in the chair next to his desk.

He was sitting almost beside me, facing his computer and typing away. "I can come back later if you're busy," I said.

"No, it's fine. What's up?" he asked as he continued to tap away at his keyboard.

I was a bit annoyed, but I started to explain what was going on, and how frustrated I was feeling.

"Damn," he muttered as he bashed away at the delete button. "Go on."

"As I was saying," I started again, sitting forward trying to get his attention. At that point his phone rang and he instantly picked it up. "I'll come back later," I said as I got up and walked out.

He nodded and waved, with a half smile and a shrug, as if he couldn't help what had just happened.

Now that really was extreme, but it did happen. To a lesser extent, many leaders listen, but they are formulating the responses in their minds as you speak.

How does listening build trust?

1. We all have a need to be respected. When someone really listens, it demonstrates that respect for us as a human being. Doctors, counselors, coaches, and many salespeople have this ability.
2. Listening is enhanced when you put yourself in the other person's shoes—being caring and empathetic— which are qualities of a trustworthy person.
3. Listening can open your mind to new ideas and concepts, and it is a great way to learn about others and, in turn, about yourself.

Being open and transparent, you'll remember, are qualities inherent in trustworthiness.

4. If you ask someone for his or her time to discuss something, you expect that individual to listen.

5. Such comments as "My door is always open" or "We'll meet weekly to discuss your work" are implicit promises that leaders will listen.

ARE YOU A TRUSTWORTHY LEADER?

As we've seen throughout this chapter, being a trustworthy leader takes dedication to leadership mastery. I've taken some of Mandy's key points and added them to the Trustworthy Person Model* to form these questions to get you thinking about how trustworthy you are as a leader.

Do this quick assessment and check your score at the end. Rate each question on the scale of 1 to 5:

1 = almost never

2 = rarely

3 = sometimes

4 = frequently

5 = almost always

Then tally your score.

Openness and Transparency	
I am open to ideas and suggestions from others in my business/team	1 2 3 4 5
I let people know if I am having a bad day or something is bothering me	1 2 3 4 5
I share information about the business/project with my people	1 2 3 4 5
Score (Total of all questions)	

Honesty and with Integrity	
I give my people the facts, so they can deal with reality	1 2 3 4 5
I treat my people fairly	1 2 3 4 5
I only reward good performers	1 2 3 4 5
Score (Total of all questions)	

Genuine and Authentic	
As a leader I am true to my core beliefs and values	1 2 3 4 5
I am clear in my own mind about what is important to me	1 2 3 4 5
My own values and the company's values are aligned	1 2 3 4 5
Score (Total of all questions)	

Courageous and Decisive	
I consider options then make a decision with conviction	1 2 3 4 5
I stand up for what I believe is the right way to treat all stakeholders	1 2 3 4 5
I admit when I've made a mistake	1 2 3 4 5
Score (Total of all questions)	

Reliable and Proven	
I only promise what I know I can deliver	1 2 3 4 5
I manage my people's expectations of me as a leader	1 2 3 4 5
I deliver on my promises	1 2 3 4 5
Score (Total of all questions)	

Caring and Empathetic	
I take time to understand the expectations and needs of my people	1 2 3 4 5
I consider how my people might be feeling	1 2 3 4 5
I think about others before I make decisions that might affect them	1 2 3 4 5
Score (Total of all questions)	
Overall Score	

How did you do?

If you scored:

72–90: You are able to build trust with your people and will be seeing the results of that. Well done.

54–71: You are able to build trust some of the time, but will find it a struggle at other times. Working on the areas you scored lower on will help you. This could include talking to someone you trust to help you with suggestions for change, or getting some coaching or mentoring to help you improve your skills in building trust as a leader

37–53: You may be having some difficulty getting others to follow your lead. Getting some specific coaching to guide you as you grow and develop in leadership and focusing on your weaker scoring areas should help. Asking your subordinates specifically about what they think you could do better is a great way to build trust with them and improve yourself. Paying particular attention to the lower scoring areas and working to improve these will help you become a better, more trusted leader

18–36: You may have been placed in a leadership role before you are ready. You need to have an honest conversation with your immediate superior about getting some support in the form of coaching or mentoring, or a good leadership program to help you improve.

Download your FREE gift to help you build trust in your leadership. Go to www.entente.com.au/US_Book_gifts and download your FREE e-book *7 Truths about Trust Every Leader Needs to Know*. Check out the many resources and services at www.entente.com.au that can help you build trust in your leadership.

Now, let's take a closer look at people management with James Adonis.

14

TRUST IN PEOPLE MANAGEMENT

Few things help an individual more than to place responsibility upon him,
and to let him know that you trust him.
—Booker T. Washington, American educator and author

INTRODUCING JAMES ADONIS

I met James Adonis through the Thought Leaders program. (For details on the program, visit www.thoughtleaders.com.au.) He amazed me with his enthusiasm and passion for what he does, so I was really pleased he agreed to write this chapter for the book.

James is Australia's leading expert on employee engagement. He shows managers how to engage their employees so that they become loyal high-performers, and he shows employees how to engage themselves in the workplace so that they focus on achieving what they want.

By the time he was twenty-four, James was managing a team of a hundred. One of his major achievements was taking a team with an employee turnover rate exceeding 70 percent and reducing it to zero—where it was maintained for two years. James's articles are regularly published in many countries. He is frequently featured in the media as a thought leader on people management and is the author of *Love Your Team: How to Halve Your Employee Turnover in Less Than 90 Days!*

For more information on James, visit his Web site at www.jamesadonis. com.

Let's see what he has to say about trust and people management.

BUILDING EMPLOYEE ENGAGEMENT BY DEVELOPING TRUST

Trust plays a vital role in people management and high employee engagement, but before we talk about trust, let me ask you this question: Are you a manager or a leader? You may think there's no real difference between the two terms, but there is.

Managers create order out of complexity and uncertainty; they keep the trains running on schedule. Leaders deal effectively with ambiguity, change, and opportunity; they inspire their teams to take the trains to places they've never been before.

So, what makes a manager a good leader? I've worked with a large number of organizations and have met very many great leaders, and while each person has a unique blend of skills and attributes, they all have one thing in common: *Their employees trust them.*

Great leaders gain, through their words and actions, the respect and trust of employees and coworkers. Trust is an absolutely essential element of effective employee engagement. Effective leadership develops trust, and the result is a team of employees who are loyal, happy, and high performing. High wages, bonuses, and other extrinsic motivators don't build trust.

Trust is built through teamwork, honesty, and fairness—all demonstrated on a daily and consistent basis by the employee's direct manager and the organization. These are the two stakeholders that have the greatest influence over an employee's level of trust. Occasionally, the trust built between an employee and his or her manager can at least partly overcome lack of trust in the organization, but I've never seen the opposite occur: If employees do not trust their manager, their sense of dedication to and engagement with the organization is ruined.

What happens when employees don't trust their managers? The first result is a loss of productivity. Employees who don't trust you to make good decisions and look out for their best interests will try to do those things themselves. Instead of focusing on productivity and quality they'll focus on protecting themselves. If the situation doesn't improve, in all likelihood they'll eventually leave.

In working with managers and teams across the country, I've developed the following list of personal skills found in effective managers. How many of these traits do you have? More importantly, how many can you develop?

- Caring—Effective managers empathize with other people's needs, concerns, problems, and goals.
- Comfortable with uncertainty—Effective managers can operate in environments that are ambiguous and unclear, and can help others create order out of chaos.
- Persistence—Effective managers stay positive and focused despite obstacles and failures.
- Excellent Communication Skills—Effective managers know how to listen closely, communicate one-on-one or in large groups, and effectively present their thoughts and ideas.
- Excellent Negotiation Skills—Effective managers are constantly negotiating, both inside and outside their own area of responsibility. Good managers seek win-win outcomes; one-sided "victories" are detrimental to the long-term health of the organization.
- Sensible and even-tempered— Even in the middle of turmoil and conflict, good managers stay calm (at least on the outside) and focused on results.

- Engaging—Good managers are effective at gaining the commitment of their employees to the goals of the whole team.
- Challenging—Good managers set the bar high and also provide the right resources and training to help their teams reach those high goals.
- Self-Aware—Good managers know how their behavior, both positive and negative, affects others, and they model the behaviors they wish their employees to display.

You may or may not have all these traits. If you don't, that's okay; with time and effort, almost anyone can develop each of these skills and attributes.

If you're already a good manager, is it worth it to put in the effort to develop great management and leadership skills? Absolutely. Great people managers build trust, and more importantly, they never take that trust for granted.

Trust provides the foundation for employee engagement and retention. In organizations and workplace relationships where there is a high level of trust, managers operate with a greater level of flexibility. Not only can managers gain additional time to focus on strategic planning, their employees are more productive as well. A study conducted in 2006 by a Cornell University research team found that small businesses that granted workers more autonomy grew at more than four times the rate of those that relied on tight top-down controls. (The article, "Human Resource Management Practices and Firm Performance in Small Businesses," is available at www.gevitygroup.com.) By trusting and empowering your team, you'll increase your productivity and theirs.

Employees are also more likely to forgive a mistake if they have trust in the person who made it. One of my mentoring clients was the manager of a book manufacturing plant in Queensland, Australia. He decided to move his employees from one processing line to another in the hope of optimizing production flow and increasing overall productivity. In a team meeting his employees told him they felt it was a bad idea; nevertheless, he explained his reasoning and asked for their support.

The change didn't work out as planned. He openly admitted his mistake in a meeting with the teams involved, and the company quickly shifted the teams back to their original assignments. His teams forgave the mistake because he discussed his reasoning before the change was made and more importantly, because he admitted his mistake and took immediate action to correct it.

Effective managers never take trust for granted because when trust exists, almost anything is easier to achieve. Building trust is the single most important task a manager has: If your team doesn't trust you, no amount of education, training, or management skills will overcome that lack of trust; if your team trusts you, there's no limit to how successful they can be.

Trust is built on expectations, needs, and promises, both with an employee's direct manager and with the organization. First let's look at the expectations, needs, and promises between a direct manager and an employee. Then we'll look at the role those elements play between employees and the organization.

TRUST BETWEEN A DIRECT MANAGER AND AN EMPLOYEE

Trust between a direct manager and an employee plays a major role in virtually all aspects of employee engagement. Results of a study in 1997 conducted by C. Ken Weidner as part of his doctoral studies at the University of Illinois–Chicago revealed that a manager's skill in developing relationships which reduce or eliminate distrust have a positive impact on employee turnover. He feels that turnover may be a result of organizations that have failed to "draw people in." Weidner also found that trust in a supervisor positively relates to higher individual performance. In other words, trust built between an employee and his or her manager results in lower turnover, higher engagement, and higher performance. That trust, and those positive outcomes, can be maintained only if expectations, needs, and promises are met.

Expectations

Here's some unsettling news: There's a conversation going on among your team members, and you're probably not a part of it. Worse yet, the conversation is about you.

Your employees analyze your decisions, your actions, and your statements. They frequently speculate about your motives and your intentions—and you may have no idea what they're saying. Hopefully, you tell your employees what you think of them, but your employees aren't obligated—and may not even have the opportunity—to tell you what they think of you, and what their expectations are of you. There's no way you can meet those expectations—or, at the very least, explain why those expectations can't be met—unless you know what they are.

How can you find out what your employees expect? It's easy: ask them.

But don't ask in a general, unfocused way. If you simply ask, "What do you expect from me as a manager?" you're unlikely to get a response with any substance. Instead, be more specific. If you're discussing an employee's development plan, ask, "What can I do to help you reach these goals?" If you're providing constructive feedback about subpar performance, ask, "What things can I do to help you reach your targets?" If an employee comes to you with a problem, don't just send them away with advice; ask, "What can I do to help you solve this?" By asking how you can help, you're not only helping, you're also getting a better sense of an employee's expectations—and what you can do to meet them.

What are the main expectations that employees have of their direct managers? Here are a few of the most common.

A strong and meaningful relationship. While your employees may be disappointed if you don't agree with their ideas, if you don't feel they're ready for promotion, or if you provide performance feedback that is negative, you can still build trust by being fair, honest, and forthright. Your employees may not love you for providing constructive criticism, but they will trust you if you always tell them the truth, no matter how tough some of those truths may be.

The managers do what they say they will do. Your employees expect you to follow through on your promises. For example, let's assume you've promised an employee a temporary development assignment in another department, but for reasons out of your control, you're unable to follow through on that promise. To you the assignment may have seemed like a perk; to the employee, once offered it's become an expectation. Failing to follow through will damage the employee's trust that you'll do what you say you'll do. In this case, you can maintain that trust by explaining the situation and honestly describing why the assignment is no longer feasible. The employee may not be happy with the decision, but he or she will understand the reasons why.

Managers will show a genuine interest in the issues—both inside and outside of work—that employees are facing. No employee wants to be a "number" or a "resource." Every employee wants to be valued for his or her unique skills and contributions. Don't you? Your employees don't expect you to solve all of their problems, but they do expect you to listen and empathize.

Managers need to be credible and respected by having a high level of expertise, knowledge, and more importantly, people skills. Managers tend to be selected because they have solid technical skills: They know the tasks of the department they'll oversee. (In fact, in many organizations, the person promoted to the managerial role often has the best technical skills—not necessarily the best people skills, which are of far greater value to a team than technical skills.) If you've been transferred to the department, most of your direct reports will forgive your lack of technical skills. What employees have a harder time forgiving is a lack of people skills; they expect to be able to trust you as a leader.

Managers will uphold the organization's values, ethics, and integrity, and they have the team's best interests at heart. Your team expects to be able to depend on you. It's that simple. Violate their expectations of integrity and professionalism and you're likely to lose their trust. Every company has policies and rules; make sure you follow them and that you enforce those policies consistently. (If you're not enforcing a policy, why have the policy?)

Your team expects you to be honest, to be fair, and to treat each member with respect and dignity.

Underperforming employees will be disciplined or monitored. Your team expects you to manage the performance of other employees. When managers don't deal with an underperforming employee, they lose the support and respect of coworkers and peers who experience the results of this poor performing employee firsthand. The entire team's morale will suffer as a result, and your team will spend valuable time and energy focusing on the underperforming employee—and on the fact that you haven't taken care of the problem.

Managers do not speak negatively about an employee to other employees. Your employees have every right to expect that their personal and professional information will be kept completely confidential. I've known managers who were tempted to "leak" an employee's performance problems to other employees in the hope that the employee would "get the message." The only message received by the employee (and by the rest of the team) was that the manager could not be trusted to maintain confidentiality and professionalism.

Needs

As with expectations, you can't meet the needs of your employees if you don't know what those needs are. In the next section, we'll look at a number of basic needs common to almost all employees, regardless of the industry they're in. But each employee is also an individual and will have individual needs. Meeting employee needs helps create engaged and empowered work teams. How do you find out what your employees need? The answer, again, is simple: ask them.

Some companies use formal surveys to get input. The advantage of a formal survey is that feedback can be confidential; the disadvantage is that you don't get to ask questions to help you understand input that's unclear. Other companies hold team meetings. The advantage of team meetings is that ideas can be openly discussed; the disadvantage is that some team members will feel reluctant to participate. A third option is to talk to employees individually.

What's the best option? In my opinion, it's best to use all three. You'll have a better chance of getting open input from your entire team, and even more important, you'll be doing what every great manager does: communicating—frequently—with your team.

What are the main needs that employees have from their direct managers? Here are a few of the most common.

Career development. Each employee deserves a chance to advance within the organization. In order to advance, employees need specific development plans based on their current skills and qualifications to help them reach their career goals. Employees need your help to receive additional training, attend seminars, receive temporary assignments to other departments, and, most of all, get constructive and objective feedback about their progress toward their career goals.

Feedback (consistently, constructively, timely). If your feedback primarily consists of yearly evaluations, it's not enough. Employees need to know and trust that they'll receive feedback, both formally and informally, on a consistent basis. In fact, I use this simple guideline: If any comment, no matter how small, on an employee's formal evaluation comes as a surprise to the employee, you as the manager have not done your job. A formal evaluation should simply be a summary of feedback given throughout the evaluation period. Your employees need to know how they're doing, and they need to hear it from you.

Work-life balance, encouraged the by manager. Some employees have incredible work ethics, and they will literally give their all to the organization. That dedication, while admirable, in the long-term is not helpful to the organization or especially to the employee. Your employees need your help in monitoring their work-life balance, and they'll need you to step in when the balance is unhealthy. They'll appreciate you've noticed how hard they're working, but they'll love the fact that you care enough about them as individuals to encourage a healthier balance.

Communication (free-flowing, frequent, two-way). Do you talk to your employees more than you listen? Your employees need to hear from you what's going on in the department and in the organization, but more importantly, they need you to listen to them. Employees also need to be able to trust they can speak honestly and without fear of recrimination. You may not agree with all their ideas, and that's okay—as long as you explain why you don't agree, and you do so in a constructive fashion. Employees need to be heard, and hearing means you must take the time to actively listen.

Honesty. If honesty is a value that is quickly forgotten when challenges or crises occur, reevaluate your priorities. Being dishonest may produce short-term results, but I can guarantee it will produce long-term distrust you may never repair.

PROMISES

Managers make promises: some intentional, or explicitly, and some unintentional, or implicitly. You make an intentional promise when you tell an employee you'll get them an assignment to work on a project in another department.

You can also make implicit promises, even if that's not your intent. For example, let's say your team is under a tight deadline and you need an employee to work overtime. Many managers might get on the phone and say, "John, we've got a dilemma. I'd really appreciate it if you could stay late. You can? Great! Thanks. I appreciate you helping me out." That could be taken as an implied promise that there's something to come, some kind of thanks or reward, just through the use of the words "I'd really appreciate it if you."

If you don't come through on your promises, both explicit and implicit, your employees will lose trust in you as a manager. Sometimes, due to company or marketplace changes, you won't be able to follow through on your promises. If you can't, don't ignore the situation. Explain what has changed and why you can't. The employee may not like what you have to say, but they will respect your honesty.

What are the main promises—either explicit or implicit—that managers make to their direct reports? Here are a few of the most common.

Managers will foster their employees' growth and development. Employees need targeted career development plans, and good leaders fulfill their promise to provide that development. Engaged employees feel they can grow within the organization; a good leader promises to provide opportunities for that growth.

Office politics will not get in the way of what is fair, right, and just. Every organization has its own unique blend of conflicting agendas, territorialism, and internal competition. As a leader, you promise to treat employees fairly and ethically in spite of office politics. Your employees expect you to stand behind them and take their side when necessary. A good leader builds trust by promising to do what's right even when—especially when—doing the right thing is the hardest thing.

The employee will be consulted from time to time on his or her opinions, thoughts, and feedback on a wide range of organizational issues. Employees don't expect you to act on all their opinions, but they do need and expect the opportunity to be heard. As a leader, you should actively solicit thoughts and feedback; while you may not always hear what you want to hear, you may be surprised by the great ideas and input you'll get. A leader promises to communicate with and, more importantly, listen to his or her team; a great leader follows through on that promise.

Managers will be reliable and consistent in how they treat employees. If your organization has rules and guidelines, make sure everyone follows them. If you can't apply a rule consistently, the rule probably should be changed.

Managers will be committed to the team and will lead by example. Employees look to their managers to set the tone for the organization. Employees expect their managers to lead, by their words and—sometimes more importantly—by their actions. As a manager, not only is what you say and do important; how you act is critical too. Employees respond to the subtlest of leadership behaviors; make sure you're a leader employees can model their own behaviors after.

Kurt Dicks, assistant professor at Simon Fraser University, studied the impact of trust in college basketball teams. After surveying players on thirty teams, he determined that players on successful teams were significantly more likely to trust their coach. Players on successful teams were more likely to believe their coach knew what was required for them to win. They believed the coach had their best interests at heart, and they believed the coach came through on what he promised. (The article, "Trust Rules: The Most Important Secret About Trust," is available at www.About.com.) By meeting employee expectations and needs, and by keeping your promises to your employees, your teams will feel a greater sense of engagement and will deliver higher performance.

TRUST BETWEEN EMPLOYEES AND THE ORGANIZATION

"You can love the organization, but the organization can't love you back." Do you agree with this contentious statement? While you may not agree with that statement in all (or any) cases, what any organization can and should provide are the three pillars of employee trust: Meeting its employees' expectations and needs and delivering on its promises. No matter how strong the bond of trust is between an employer and his or her manager, employees must have a high level of trust in the organization in order to reach their potential.

Expectations

Employment is a two-way street in every organization: The organization has expectations of its employees, but just as importantly, the employees have expectations of the organization. To reach your team's goals, you make your expectations clear so employees know what to do and how to do it. But if your organization doesn't know what employees expect, how can it meet those expectations?

We'll look at some of the more common expectations that apply to most industries in a moment. The list is a great start for understanding employee expectations. If you want to know what employees in your particular organization expect, the best tools to use are surveys, group feedback meetings, and suggestion boxes. Since expectations employees have of the organization tend to be more general in nature, surveys and group meetings are a great way to get feedback from your staff.

What are the main expectations that employees have of the organization? Here are a few of the most common.

Maintain a strong and positive reputation among customers and the community. Employees expect to be proud of the job they do, but they also expect to be proud of their organization. An organization that stands behind its products or services and builds ties with the community is an organization employees will be proud of.

Document and adhere to fair and equitable personnel practices. It's not enough to simply have policies in place; employees expect those policies to be enforced fairly and consistently. One of my consulting clients is an organization that had sales executives who were not required to follow expense report policies: The company felt that keeping salespersons "happy" was more important than applying policies consistently. Other employees were disciplined while salespersons were not; as a result, trust between employees and the company was broken. Employees assume that rules are in place for a reason, and they expect those rules to be applied consistently to everyone.

Pay levels and workplace conditions will be on par and competitive with the rest of the market. Most employees don't expect their organizations to pay the highest wages, but they do expect their wages to be competitive so they can feel they are being treated fairly. (Keep in mind that while higher wages will certainly be appreciated, research clearly shows that high wages do not automatically ensure high employee engagement; on the other hand, developing trust between employees and their managers and the organization will absolutely create higher employee engagement.)

Align the organization's values with those of the employees. Employees who feel the company pays lip service to its mission statement or stated goals quickly lose trust; employees expect to be asked to perform in a manner consistent with the organization's goals and values. As we'll discuss in a moment, providing outstanding customer service is on the list of most organizations' core values, and employees expect the organization to treat its employees with the same courtesy and respect given to customers.

Encourage and ensure that all employees focus on quality and customer satisfaction. Every organization provides a product or service. Encouraging the best possible quality and service proves to customers and —just as importantly—to employees that the organization acts with integrity. If the organization doesn't fulfill promises to customers, how can employees expect the company to fulfill its promises to them?

Needs

Understanding needs is just as important as understanding expectations. To find out what your employees need from the organization, you can use tools like surveys, group meetings, individual meetings, or simple informal conversations. It never hurts to ask, and you never know what you might learn. Even if a discussion doesn't yield any input you can use, your employees will appreciate the fact that you've asked and that you're communicating with them.

What are the main needs that employees have of the organization? Here are a few of the most common.

A secure and stable organization that is not at risk of liquidation or downsizing. Years ago, employees may have felt they had a job for life. Today, however, the rapidly changing global economy makes that promise impossible. On the other hand, employees do need to feel the company is doing everything possible to stay healthy and strong. Employees will quickly lose trust in the organization if they feel other goals, like an executive's or an owner's personal enrichment, are more important. Employees are savvy enough to understand and accept that business conditions change, but they need to feel the organization is actively working to positively adapt and react to changes in the marketplace that could put the organization at risk.

A focus on health and safety. Employees need to feel valued and respected; a consistent and proactive focus on healthy and safe working conditions as preventative measures demonstrates every employee's importance and worth.

A visible and accessible CEO and executive team who share as much information about the organization's performance, plans, and goals as possible. Communication is critical to building engagement, and employees need consistent contact with the leadership team in order to build trust in their leadership.

Creating a winning and successful team, thereby enhancing the trust an employee has for the organization. Success breeds success, and employees need to feel they're part of a successful team. Morale—and trust—suffers greatly when a team or an organization is unsuccessful. Is it possible for every team to succeed? Probably not. And if that's the case, then communication is critical to maintaining morale, engagement, and trust.

A front-line management team with a high degree of emotional intelligence that builds positive relationships with employees. In a business setting, emotional intelligence is a person's sense of self-awareness, altruism, personal motivation, empathy, and the ability to care. Leaders who possess high emotional intelligence build flourishing careers and lasting, meaningful relationships. Great leaders have solid technical skills, but they also have outstanding interpersonal skills and are able to build trust throughout the organization.

Pay will be reasonably in line with similar positions in other organizations. Most employees don't expect to be the highest paid in the company, but they do need to feel their pay level is fair. There needs to be a consistent approach to determining salary levels across the organization. The more employees understand about the process for determining salaries, the more easily they can put their wage levels into context.

Performance and hard work will be recognized. Do you appreciate it when your boss thanks you for your efforts? Of course you do. All of us need recognition and praise. Your employees need that recognition too. What's a simple way to start recognizing your employees? Say, "Thank you." Catch them doing something right, and praise them for it. The possibilities for meeting your employees' need for recognition are limitless.

Promises

Managers make explicit and implicit promises, and so do organizations. An organization that fails to live up to those promises creates distrust.

The biggest promise an organization should make, both explicitly and by action, is that it will communicate openly and honestly with its employees. If promises can't be met, employees deserve to know why.

What are the main promises the organization should make to its employees? Here are a few of the most common.

Promotions will be based on merit, and employee performance will determine rewards and recognition. A few years ago an employee, upset with being passed over for promotion, said to me, "This isn't fair. I'm the most senior employee." I responded, "Seniority is important, but what's important is that it's given you the chance to be the most skilled and qualified employee in the department. You haven't taken advantage of that opportunity in the past, but I've put together a development plan that can get you there if you put in the effort." Fairness is critical to building employee trust, and basing rewards on merit creates the fairest system possible.

The organization's culture aligns with its values, and those values are demonstrated and promoted each and every day. Does your organization promote an open door policy where employees are supposed to feel free to speak to any member of management, yet somehow the management team is never available? Values are important, but the culture of the organization must align with those values. Do you want your employees to treat customers with respect and dignity? Start by treating your employees with respect and dignity. When your culture supports your business values, trust is just one of the positive results.

The organization sees its employees as valuable assets and invests in and nurtures those assets. Almost every company has a mission statement or values statement that asserts something along the lines of, "Our employees are our most valuable asset," but the company's actions speak louder than words. For example, if your company has ineffective safety programs, a culture that creates a poor work-life balance, or non-existent training and development initiatives, how valued will your employees feel? Promoting from within whenever possible is a great way to show that the organization values its employees. By developing the skills of employees, the organization fulfils its promise to encourage, support, and foster the growth of the organization and of each individual.

The organization will be transparent in terms of why certain decisions are made and why changes occur. While employees may not play a role in making certain decisions, most will want to understand why those decisions were made, especially if the resulting change directly affects them. If you need to change work hours, for example, explain why the decision was made and why the change is important for the health of the organization. I often tell managers, "If you can't explain it or justify it, then you shouldn't do it." Again, your employees may not agree with the decision, but at least they'll understand the reasoning behind it, and they'll be able to trust that you'll share your thoughts and logic with them.

Employee benefits will be maintained. Businesses experiencing poor financial results often make cuts in employee benefits, usually with disastrous effect. Why? Benefit cuts signal a lack of commitment to an employee. Cutting expense accounts, limiting travel, or making cuts in nonessential areas is easy for an employee to understand on a logical basis, whereas making cuts to benefits feels personal and breaks promises made.

Developing a greater sense of trust among employees and managers and the organization should be high on every organization's list of objectives. Only 51 percent of employees who responded to Watson Wyatt's research report "WorkUSA 2004/2005: Effective Employees Drive Financial Results," however, said they "have trust and confidence in their senior management." The survey also found that only 50 percent of workers "believe what management tells them."

Effective employee engagement begins with trust. If you want a team of engaged, high-performing employees, build trust by ensuring that your employees' needs and expectations are met and that you and your organization keeps promises that are made. Fall short in any one of those areas, and you'll damage that sense of trust; maintain each, and there's no limit to what you and your organization can achieve.

WHAT TO DO WHEN TRUST BREAKS DOWN

In a perfect world, your employees will always trust you and your organization. In spite of your best efforts, though, trust can and will erode. That's the bad news. The good news is you can recover. How do you rebuild trust?

1. Communicate openly. Talk about the situation. Describe any mistakes you've made, what you've learned from those mistakes, and what you'll do in the future. Don't be afraid to share bad news and to admit mistakes. Explain the rationale behind decisions you've made, and encourage employees to give input and feedback on decisions you make. Most importantly, accept feedback with grace and act professionally at all times. Rebuilding trust takes time. The old cliché "It takes ten pats on the back to overcome one kick in the rear" is especially true when you've lost the trust of your employees.

2. Make changes based on employee input. Listen to your employees and implement good suggestions. Some managers are hesitant to act on employee input because they feel all the ideas should be theirs. Great managers realize they don't have all the answers. What matters most is that you make positive changes; it doesn't matter where the ideas for those changes come from. Employees who know you'll listen and act on their ideas will regain their trust in you.

3. Make sure your employees fully understand your expectations. In order for employees to be effective, they have to know what their job is and how to do their job. Employees who make mistakes will often blame their manager for not setting clear expectations, and as a result, they will lose trust in that manager. While that may not seem fair, it's also a fact of life: Most of us are initially defensive when we make a mistake. Setting clear expectations not only helps employees perform better but also creates an environment of trust.

4. Hold employees accountable. If you've made a mistake that eroded trust, that doesn't mean you shouldn't hold your

employees accountable for their mistakes. Rewarding high performers and holding poor performers accountable through discipline and termination builds an environment of trust.

5. "Cast the right shadow." Employees look to their managers to set the tone for the organization; they expect the company leaders to lead in word and in action. What you say and do as a manager is important; how you say and do things is critical, too, because your team will scrutinize everything you do, especially if trust has been broken. By being a great role model and constantly casting the right shadow, you set an example for your employees to follow, and they'll also place their trust in you.

I'd like to specifically highlight two areas here that James so capably addressed.

The first is the concept of seeking feedback from employees and engaging them, through surveys and other means, in the direction of the business. One of the things I have seen time and time again in companies is the well-meaning employee opinion survey followed by…nothing! I once worked for an organization that conducted such a survey, and the months went by with no communication of the results. When I quizzed my manager on it, he admitted that the results were so bad that senior management decided not to release them!

Why bother asking if you are not going to do anything about it? One of the things I tell people who look at doing the Entente Trust Survey is that they have to promise they will take action on the areas showing low levels of trust. If the commitment is not there, I tell them not to bother, and certainly not to do the survey. I certainly don't want my name associated with a "survey that didn't work."

What happens when a company surveys its employees?

1. It creates expectations that since it is asking for employees' opinions, it will do something as a result. When nothing happens, the expectation is not met.

2. There is an implicit promise made along the same lines, unless it is clearly stated that the only reason the survey is being done is to see how the company measures up against its competitors (which is the reality in many cases).
3. The need for respect is met in conducting the survey, but then it is not met when the opinions are not listened to.

The communication surrounding the survey needs to be managed very well so that expectations about what is likely to happen, and when, are managed properly. The best thing to do is get everyone involved. When you release the results, get your people involved in determining the best solutions and ways of improving the areas that rated poorly. As was demonstrated in the Fantastic Furniture story, everyone has something of value to add, if you just listen.

The second thing I want to point out is James's comment about disciplining underperforming employees. We've all seen it. The couple of people who have been slack and not pulled their weight, or the people who got the job done but left a trail of destruction in their wake. When these people are rewarded just like everyone else, it blows all the good things the leaders might have done before.

I was at a breakfast not that long ago and someone told a story about how the manager had bought a few books of movie vouchers to give out as rewards throughout the year. One day she checked them and realized that they were, unfortunately, about to expire that week. As a result, she gave them out to all the staff. *All the staff.* That is not reward and recognition. That's poor management.

There is a fine line between equity and fairness in the workplace, between reward and recognition for performance. If you build a performance-based system, stick to it. By having the system, you have created expectations and have made promises—some explicit and some implicit—about how people will be treated. It does take courage to be able to give constructive feedback to an employee who is underperforming, but I can guarantee that the rest of your people will be watching you like a hawk to see that it is done, and they will trust you more for it. It meets their needs for security and for fairness and respect.

ENPS FOR DIRECT MANAGERS

James gave us a great outline of ENPs for managers who have people reporting to them. He also talked about ENPs employees have of the organizations they are employed by, as well as those of their managers. The following questions look only at what you need to be doing as a direct manager.

Do this quick assessment and check your score at the end. Rate each question on the scale of 1 to 5:

1 = almost never

2 = rarely

3 = sometimes

4 = frequently

5 = almost always

Then tally your score.

Direct Manager ENPs®	
1. I ask my people what they expect of me as a manager	1 2 3 4 5
2. I take time to develop relationships with my people	1 2 3 4 5
3. I provide constructive feedback to my people	1 2 3 4 5
4. I do what I say I'm going to do	1 2 3 4 5
5. I have a genuine interest in my people, in and out of work	1 2 3 4 5
6. I actively develop my management and people skills	1 2 3 4 5
7. I behave congruently with the company's values	1 2 3 4 5
8. I take action with under-performing employees	1 2 3 4 5
9. I keep information about each employee confidential	1 2 3 4 5
10. I help my people develop their careers	1 2 3 4 5
11. I encourage work-life balance	1 2 3 4 5
12. I communicate with my people two-way (I listen as well as speak)	1 2 3 4 5
13. I make sure that my people are treated fairly	1 2 3 4 5
14. I involve my people in business ideas and decisions	1 2 3 4 5
15. I walk the talk	1 2 3 4 5
Overall score	

How did you do?

If you scored:

   60–75: Your team should be performing well in response to your good management and trust. Well done.

   45–59: You are getting it right some of the time. Take a look at the areas you need to improve on and think about what you can do differently.

20–44: You may have an underperforming team and therefore need to work on building trust. Take a look at the areas you need to improve on and create an action plan—today!

15–19: Your team may not be responding to you as their manager, and it is likely that you are frustrated. Ask your immediate manager right now for some coaching or support on how to build trust.

Download your FREE gift to help you build trust in your people management. Go to www.entente.com.au/US_Book_gifts and download your FREE e-book *7 Truths about Trust Every People Manager Needs to Know*. Check out the many resources and services at www.entente.com.au that can help you build trust in your people management.

Now, let's look at trust from a different angle, trust in branding and marketing, with Fiona Pearman.

15

TRUST IN MARKETING AND BRANDING

People are not going to switch from their trusted brand to a new and similar brand without good reason. This is why follow-on products constantly face an uphill battle when coming to market.
—Eric Bolesh, Research Manager, Cutting Edge Information

INTRODUCING FIONA PEARMAN

I was actually introduced to Fiona Pearman by David Penglase, who wrote the next chapter, on sales. Fiona has worked with David for a number of years providing marketing advice and a strategic framework for building the equity and reputation of David's brands.

Fiona's approach to strategic brand management is holistic and organic. Her passion is to work with clients who recognize the strategic value of consistently managing their brand to build brand equity and reputation in the marketplace. She is dedicated to providing realistic, insightful tactics, which deliver tangible changes and results.

Fiona worked as a senior marketer and brand development manager for several international brands prior to establishing a boutique consultancy, Brand Management Strategies, in 1999.Her approach includes a thorough understanding of the business model and objectives, an in-depth analysis of the client experience, consideration of how to best position and leverage the brand offering, and appropriate marketing tactics to achieve the desired business outcomes. (For more information on her company, visit www. brandillumination.com.au.)

WHAT DO WE MEAN BY MARKETING AND BRANDING?

Branding is far more than a logo, the packaging, or an advertising campaign. It is at the heart of every business and must be aligned with the organization's business strategy to ensure that at every opportunity the brand is interacting positively with its customers and other stakeholders.

Marketing is both the messages and the communication channels we choose to take the brand to the marketplace.

Every interaction with your brand will have a positive or a negative effect in terms of how the customer perceives the brand. The job of branding and marketing is to provide a path that maximizes positive brand interactions.

We're All Intuitive Brand Experts

We all interact with brands and marketing messages every day. In a way, we are all experts when it comes to knowing what we like and don't like, and what we trust and don't trust when it comes to selecting products and services. In fact, we often choose certain brands because they enhance or reinforce the image we have of ourselves. While we all have this intuitive sense of what we trust in brands and marketing, this section provides a framework for evaluating the role of trust in branding and marketing.

WHAT ARE OUR MOST TRUSTED BRANDS AND WHY DO WE TRUST THEM?

According to a Reader's Digest 2007 survey, Australia's top five most trusted brands are Cadbury, Panadol, Band-aid, Colgate, and Sony. These five were all "trust leaders" within their category.

Think of brands you interact with every day: your choice of coffee or tea, your breakfast cereal, your deodorant, your car, your telephone provider. You're not even thinking about many of these items because you inherently trust they will perform as you expect them to and as they have performed for you in the past.

How Brands Meet Our Needs

Making an emotional connection with their customers. While consistent quality is extremely important, brands that create a buzz and have high referral rates make a great effort to create an emotional connection with their customers. Repeatedly using a particular brand is like belonging to a tribe or a club: Customers like the brand because they feel it enhances an aspect of their own identity. Think of the choices we make with regard to fashion labels, watches, cars, and restaurants: What we wear, what we drive, and where we go say something about who we are, and we make the choice that fits our self-perception.

Alma Stanonik, former brand manager for Mont Blanc, comments: "People become emotionally attached to their pens. They trust and like them. We have customers that come in and say things like 'this used to be my grandfather's pen.' We have a German customer [who] has thirty pens, and some of them [are] sixty years old."

People connect with brands to meet other, deeper needs. The challenge is to be able to identify what those varied needs are in order to market products and services in a way that meets those.

Continually building and improving quality. It is no longer enough to consistently provide good quality; today's marketplace and customers demand that the products and services they use be continually refined, upgraded, and improved. Competition is tough, and successful brands recognize the need to increamntally enhance their offer.

Remaining relevant and encouraging customer interaction. In an era of information overload, enormous choice and rapid technological change, trusted brands ensure they evolve with the times. They regularly assess and measure their products' performance and their brand's appeal. They also invite feedback and creativity from their customers to ensure that what they offer is both relevant and meaningful to their customer base. [Customer involvement is covered in more detail in Iven Frangi's chapter on customer experience.]

Being relevant is also about encouraging a dynamic brand culture throughout the organization—a culture that is responsive to change and innovative in solving problems.

Having clarity and being confident. Each brand needs to have a clear positioning strategy that defines what it stands for, who it serves, what its vision and values are, and how it is differentiated from the competition. Once these are defined, the brand doesn't have to try to be relevant or meaningful to everybody; rather, they know they do a good job for a particular group of customers, who appreciate what they offer. They confidently address a need, meet expectations, and over time, build trust with their target market.

How Brands Manage Our Expectations

Building their reputation for trust over time. By consistently providing quality products and experiences, companies secure customer loyalty. Customers learn that they can trust the brand because it is reliable and dependable. We learn to trust that our favorite chocolate bar will taste the same or that a charity we donate to is consistently doing good work and managing their funds well.

As Amanda Young, Executive Director of the Australian Centre for Retail Studies, explains in her article "Australia's Most Trusted Brands" (*Readers*

Digest, June 2006), "We have greater trust in brands that evoke positive memories over a long period, and that constantly do what we need them to do."

Providing simplicity in a busy world. Trusted brands enable us to make clear choices in an information-overloaded world. From which toothpaste to select at the supermarket to where to take a partner for a special dinner, we rely on past brand knowledge and experiences to help us easily make the choice that is right for us. Imagine if we had to evaluate every option every time we wanted to buy a product or use a service! We would never get anything else done. Trusted brands allow us to cut through the clutter and keep moving forward.

In a sense, successful brands create their own high benchmark in terms of expectations: Once we have experienced something we like, we reasonably expect that a particular product or service will continue to perform at that level. There is no room for complacency, or any slackening of product quality or service levels.

Listening to their stakeholders. By establishing a "marketing feedback loop," all stakeholders—including customers and employees—are able to provide the valuable information that can improve and fine-tune the marketing message or offer. Frontline or customer service staff are an often neglected resource that can provide great insight in terms of the effectiveness, interest, and suitability of an offer for the target customers.

Customers themselves need an easy way to provide both positive and negative feedback, much of which can be utilized to improve the organization's ability to manage customer expectations. This knowledge is fed into a process to continually improve the outcomes of each marketing campaign.

How Brands Keep Promises

Ensuring they have the systems, processes, and people to deliver on what their brand has promised. Trusted brands deliver on criteria that are important to you, such as taste, value for money, and speed or ease of use. Brands make promises regularly through their taglines and with specific marketing campaigns. While having a good product is important, the strongest brands ensure that they live up to their promises at every point of customer interaction.

Understanding stakeholder expectations and needs for branding and marketing. The ways in which brands can keep their promises to both internal and external stakeholders are outlined in the following sections.

Internal Stakeholders

All internal stakeholders rely on the organization as a whole to deliver on its brand promise and marketing messages. In fact all internal stakeholders are interdependent in ensuring that delivery: They each have a role to play, and each group must be trusted to do their part in creating a positive brand experience.

Internal brand management and marketing. Most organizations need greater integration. Internal brand management forces organizations to get rid of the silos and ensure that the left hand and the right hand fully understand their contribution to delivering the brand promise.

Equally as important as external branding and marketing activities aimed at customers, internal marketing is critical to informing and inspiring all the internal stakeholders to collectively manage the expectations, meet the needs, and keep the promises made to the customers.

This interdependence across all facets of the organization requires trust: Each division within the organization must fulfill its part in creating that positive brand experience. Failure at any point along the production, sales, and delivery line can break down trust.

Whole of organization approach. Brands are trusted when they consistently deliver on their brand promise and their marketing messages. Delivering the brand depends on the whole organization understanding what the brand stands for and their part in creating a memorable brand experience.

Everyone within the organization needs to have a high level of "brand literacy": that is, they understand their role and the behaviors required to deliver on the brand promise and to live up to the marketing messages.

To trust each other, all divisions throughout the organization must believe in the brand vision and values. Everyone needs to receive information and be invited to provide feedback on marketing campaigns. Frontline personnel, such as call center, retail, and sales staff, rely on this information so they can present an informed and trustworthy response to inquiries generated through the marketing campaigns.

Trust must also extend to operational, consulting, and manufacturing staff. Again, these employees must be inspired by the brand promise and informed of the marketing campaigns so they understand that they are being trusted to deliver a product or service of a certain quality, within a certain time frame.

Trust internally ultimately manifests to trust externally. When all divisions of the organization get it right and the customer has a great experience that lives up to their expectations and meets their needs, trust is established, and it will likely lead to repeat business and referrals.

The "employer brand" and the fight for talent. Another significant aspect to internal brand management and marketing is the growing shortage of talent. Many large corporations are reporting difficulty in attracting and retaining the best staff. By focusing on their "employer brand," organizations can create a culture which lives up to the expectations and needs of its staff, whether that means flexible work hours, tuition assistance, or additional benefits, to name but a few.

One of the outcomes of becoming an "employer of choice" is that the organization is likely to achieve positive press coverage, thus attracting still more candidates, and staff are likely to recommend their employer to friends, thereby reducing recruitment costs.

External Stakeholders

Customers. As we've already discussed, brands must meet the needs of their customers while managing their customers' expectations and keeping the promises they make to them.

While customer trust is imperative to an organization's long-term survival, other, external stakeholders and relationships likewise rely on trust.

The general public. Even when they are not actual customers, it is good to engender general recognition of your brand as a worthwhile contributor to the community, a reputable employer, and a brand they can trust, should they ever need your product or service.

Suppliers. An organization that explains its brand promise and marketing campaign to its suppliers involves those suppliers in their part of creating trust with customers. This, in turn, highlights the need for a trusting relationship between the supplier and the organization, which subsequently leads to being able to arrange favorable trading terms, suitable delivery schedules, and a harmonious relationship.

The media. Members of the media need to be able to trust that an organization's spokespeople will speak the truth and inform them honestly of any positive or negative developments. The media can be a great ally to a trusted brand. On the other hand, an organization that does not tell the truth will eventually be found out, which can be much more damaging and will erode brand trust.

HOW DO ORGANIZATIONS GENERATE, PROMOTE, AND BUILD TRUST WITH BRANDING AND MARKETING?

Here are thirteen key things that organizations should be focusing on to build trust in the branding and marketing of their company, products, and services.

Media Fragmentation and Trust—the Dawning of Customer-Controlled Advertising

The types of media and communication channels chosen by their target market will increasingly determine which media channels marketers select.

Customers not only have a huge selection of products and services from which to choose, they also have an ever-increasing range of media from which to source information and entertainment. These additional media options reduce the time in which customers are receiving such traditional media as free to air TV, radio, and mainstream newspapers and magazines.

With banner ads, pop-ups, video streaming, and ads for products and services within computer games, there are more and more places to display the brand and voice the marketing messages.

CEOs and CFOs are very focused on providing a measurable return on investment. This is forcing marketers to cleverly analyze which media will prove most effective in building the brand's reputation and increasing revenue.

The implications for marketers are vital: They must be able to determine which marketing sources their target markets regularly use and which they rely on for knowledge or information. As marketing consultant Kim Brooks notes in her online article "Marketing: It's a Trust Game" (February 19, 2001): "Marketing has now become a trust game. Consumers will listen to sources that they trust: media, friends, and brands they trust. Because these are the entities that won't yell at them, slick them or spin them, they simply pass on relevant, accurate information (at least that's the perception)."

Actions Speak Louder Than Words

As ad agency George Patterson Y&R noted in reporting their "brand asset evaluator" research for 2006, "Consumers are increasingly seeking brands which 'do' rather than 'are.'" It is no longer enough to be known for something; brands must actively demonstrate, at every possible moment and via new products, that they truly are friendly, exciting, knowledgeable, fun—or whatever they define as their brand values.

Those brands that do—that is, they innovate, create, and provide quirky, memorable marketing messages—are the ones that sustain customer trust, because by stretching their appeal, they are saying: "I am worth trusting for the long term. You won't get bored with me. I will grow and develop and stay relevant to your life."

Honesty When Things Go Wrong

Sometimes organizations are tempted to try to cover up something that is unpalatable about their behavior. For example, in 2005 James Hardie (a self-professed "world leader in fiber cement siding and backerboard") initially provided fewer funds than were needed to satisfy asbestos claims. Such behavior does not build long-term trust.

In contrast, organizations such as Arnott's and Masterfoods, which each proactively dealt with a business-threatening situation due to alleged product tampering, were rewarded with increased loyalty once the crisis was over. As Brand Manager Simon Brommell explained in 2005 after Masterfoods reacted quickly and destroyed millions of Mars Bars in the interest of public safety: "Trust played an important role. Consumers want to know about a company, what it believes in. What does the brand stand for beyond profits? What is the emotional proposition? Consumers are looking for transparency—they hold this at a fundamental level. Can I trust you to do what you say?"

Expectation of Customer Involvement

In a world where anyone can create a negative Web site or blog that details their unhappy customer experience, marketers working to build their brand's reputation need to encourage and respond to a two-way dialogue with both happy and not-so-happy customers.

Well-managed customer feedback Web sites can be of great benefit to marketers, who can see by reading the candid comments whether the organization is meeting its customer's needs and expectations and delivering on its brand promise.

Additionally, customers are seeking greater involvement with the brands they know and trust. For example, online surveys and competitions and short message service (SMS) alerts and SMS voting are ways in which customers are having a say about their experience with a particular brand. In some cases, they are contributing ideas for advertising or promotion and for creating new products. This level of interactivity fosters a high level of trust between the organization and its customers. It does need to be managed well, however, for customers do not want to waste their time or feel their contribution is not appreciated.

Can Marketers Gain Gen Y tTust?

A further difficulty for marketers is the emerging Gen Y (those born between 1980 and 1995), who is now entering the workforce. These highly educated, streetwise, and very savvy young people have grown up in an era of abundant choice and brand names. They have sung along to advertising jingles as toddlers and nagged their parents for every latest fad as they were growing up. Now with their ipods, camera phones, and downloadable music and movies, they are not easily convinced by traditional advertising. In fact, Gen Y tends to be cynical about brands and marketing.

Marketers targeting Gen Y need to draw on both alternative media options and more interactive involvement (as discussed earlier). Because there are so many media options and digital devices, this age group tends to be difficult to reach. And they certainly don't believe something is true just because they saw it on TV or read it in a newspaper.

As Marketing Vox reported on February 17, 2004, in their online Media-post titled "Echo Effect: A New Generation of Media Users, Ad Distrusters": "Kids aged 12 to 24 have a declining trust in advertising, according to a new study by Yankelovich. With all the media choices and the increasing control consumers have over those choices, little patience remains for advertising (or programming) that assumes a one-way conversation."

With a low boredom threshold, Gen Y expects clever, fun messages and an opportunity to interact with the brand—on *their* terms. Many "young" brands have an edgy look and feel, advertising that can be confusing to older people, and Web sites with free games and video—all of which creates an interesting, interactive experience that is differentiated from other brands. As long as they keep adding to their content, refining their products, and offering an interesting brand experience, they will build trust and deliver on the demanding expectations of the Gen Y market.

With so many media and communication channels competing for the attention of Gen Yers, with their ability to sense and dismiss marketing hype, marketers have a significant challenge to attract them or to get across any meaningful marketing message.

Leveraging Trust for Profit—Stretching the Brand (Brand Extensions)

Not only is building trust essential to long-term brand health, it also provides an avenue for additional profit potential in the fact that it is known and trusted. Brand extensions—taking an existing brand into a new product category or service area—provides a huge opportunity for increased revenue. Of course, it is important to ensure that the new product category does not undermine the original brand's position.

One of the world's most successful stories of brand extension is Richard Branson's Virgin Group. By defining themselves as "the customer's champion," they have been able to move into diverse industries where they perceive that there is an opportunity for a new player: airlines, music, credit cards, mobile phones, and even bridal wear. As Rohan Gamble, previously the managing director of Virgin Money, said during Vanessa Hall's July 2005 interview with him, "Virgin can bring out completely different products, and customers think, 'I trust Virgin, so the product must be good.'"

Brand extension can be a powerful way to increase revenue, engage with new markets, and build reputation. However, it must be well managed, and trust is an integral part of assessing any brand extension opportunities that are identified. By utilizing the Entente Trust Model as part of the assessment criteria, an organization ensures that it will not damage or erode existing brand equity. The model encourages the organization to actively assess how the new product manages the expectations and meets the needs of the target market and to think through all the steps necessary to keeping their promises.

Choosing the Marketing Channels That Will Most Enhance Trust

As noted earlier, there are an ever-increasing number of options from which marketers must choose the best mix to increase revenue and reinforce a solid relationship between the customer and the organization. They must also think in terms of "fit"; that is, does that Web site, TV program, magazine fit with my brand and my customers?

The selection of marketing channels must be informed by an understanding of the expectations and needs of the target market(s): What is appropriate or suitable to their lifestyle?

Advertising and Trust

Over time, advertising for many products has changed from being about facts and benefits to being about creating an emotion or feeling—such as fun, excitement, calm, or friendliness.

According to InsightExpress (a self-proclaimed "leading provider of digital marketing research"), "Consumer trust in advertising has plunged 41% in the past 3 years, and only 10% of consumers say they 'trust' advertising ads today." (This is excerpted from the company's presentation at a search engine strategies conference held on February 27, 2006.)

With 90 percent of consumers lacking trust in ads, marketers are choosing quirky, humorous, and offbeat creative ideas to stand out.

Direct Marketing and Trust

Direct marketing refers to making direct contact with a potential customer. In the past, it included direct mail or telemarketing directed at either householders or businesses. Today, a large amount of direct marketing is done via the Internet and through e-mails. In fact, the huge amount of spam has led to a ban on unsolicited e-mail marketing in some countries. E-mail marketing continues to grow, nevertheless, with many organizations building an "opt-in database" where they regularly communicate information and offers to customers.

To effectively utilize this marketing option, marketers must ensure that the content and messages they send out are valuable and accurate to their customers. They must also protect their customers' data and not allow an unauthorized third party to use it. If they fall short, recipients will "opt-out," and trust in the brand will be eroded.

As John Greoo, President of the Direct Marketing Association USA, said in an address on June 21, 2006: "The best way to build confidence and trust is by demonstrating that we are responsible stewards of the marketer-consumer relationship. That means informing consumers about their choices and their rights. It means honoring their preferences, being responsive to their concerns, and safeguarding their data."

Online Advertising and Trust

Even though the Internet is a relatively new player as a media channel, it is steadily increasing its share of the marketing budget. However, research suggests that many consumers find banner ads and pop-up ads extremely annoying. According to Yankelovich Partners, a consumer research firm, in 2006 "70% actively look for ways to block, opt-out, or eliminate advertising." (This quotation was taken from the company's presentation at a search engine strategies conference held on February 27, 2006.)

This ties in with the one of the challenges cited previously: Customers want to choose their advertising and have more control over the messages they receive. By respecting and meeting this need of customers to be able to control the advertising they receive, an organization is likely to build trust and credibility.

One area that is growing is "search marketing," or the paid ads that appear alongside your search results in Internet search facilities. Because these ads are related to the search they are much more likely to be useful and relevant to the customer. A brand that wants to create positive brand experiences needs to reach customers without annoying or distracting them—thus enhancing rather than breaking down trust.

Public Relations and Trust

One of the cornerstones of gaining brand credibility is to have an active public relations program, targeted at relevant media, that works to showcase positive aspects of the brand and, in times of crisis, works to contain and manage any damage caused by scandals or sabotage.

The media have direct contact with your customers; it is therefore vitally important to be open and honest when utilizing this channel for reaching customers. As mentioned earlier, the companies that react quickly and honestly and protect customers will ultimately build trust in their brand, which will lead to greater loyalty and revenues in the long term.

Sponsorship

Whether it is the local junior football team or a national cancer program, organizations need to carefully research the right sponsorship opportunities in terms of "brand fit." If the sponsored organization is not well run and funds are mismanaged, it will reflect badly on the sponsor, which may erode trust. Some of the best sponsorships involve a direct link in terms of expertise and the sponsored program: for example, a large bank sponsoring educational programs that improve money management skills.

The stronger the link between the sponsor organization and the cause, the more alignment there will be in terms of managing the expectations of customers. If customers are asking, "Why did they sponsor that event or club?" then the link has not been explained clearly enough, and the organization runs the risk of confusing customers: in other words, not meeting their expectations.

Co-branding and Trust

Co-branding occurs when two or more brands come together to offer an enhanced product or service. For instance, Sony and Ericsson developed a camera phone together, drawing on the strengths and expertise of both organizations. Again, brand fit is very important when selecting a co-branding partner: Where both organizations command a high level of trust and respect, it is likely to work well.

However, co-branding with an organization that is not well regarded by certain markets is likely to lead to less-successful results, and it could impact negatively on both brands in terms of their reputation and trust.

Celebrity endorsement is a type of co-branding and needs to be carefully considered. In such cases, brand fit is important, as are contingency strategies if the celebrity falls from grace.

"The secret to successful co-branding is to stay true to the brand personality and values, and to choose partners carefully—partners who not only share some of those values, but [also] target similar consumer segments to which value added packages will appeal," observed Paul Temporal in his August 2001 "Branding Tips" column for www.BrandingAsia.com.

Entente's Trust Model can be a valuable tool to assist with determining the synergy between two organizations considering a co-branding opportunity. By putting the proposed product or service through the model process, with representatives from each organization, it will become obvious if there are any deficiencies in terms of managing expectations, meeting needs, or keeping promises with the target market(s).

I'd like to specifically comment on a couple of issues Fiona mentioned. The first is to take a look at what happens when consumers' needs change, from a trust perspective. This is vital to understand not only from a branding and marketing perspective but also from the perspective of innovation and product development.

Let's use another true-to-life example.

Cheryl has been using the same night cream for years. She loves the way it feels when she puts it on, loves the fragrance, and loves that it makes her skin quite smooth—which is especially significant now that she's hit the big 4-0 and is feeling a bit touchy about it! The packaging on her cream states that it helps prevent wrinkles, its active ingredients work while you sleep, and its non-greasy formula won't leave stains on the pillow. Perfect!

Let's take a look at Cheryl's ENP wall.

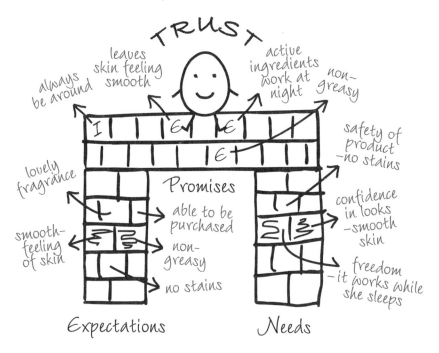

Cheryl's getting a bit low on her cream and decides to shop for more. As she walks over to the department store counter to pick up another bottle, Cheryl is greeted by a saleswoman.

"Would you like to try their new type of night cream?" she asks Cheryl.

"No thanks. I'm perfectly happy with this one."

"You do know that this new product has a special anti-aging formula that the old one doesn't?" coaxes the saleswoman. "Would you like to try a little on your hand?"

Cheryl sighs, "OK, thanks," she says, extending her hand. She notices that this cream has the same fragrance and the same smooth feel as the old cream.

She glances at the bottle. "Hmm, only $20 more, and I get the anti-aging formula as well!" she thinks. "Thanks, I'll take one of those," she says turning to the saleswoman with a satisfied smile.

What just happened? Cheryl was perfectly happy with the cream she had been using for years. What changed her mind that quickly?

A new need! A lot of women are quite sensitive to the concept of looking older. Anyone that can create a product or a service that makes us feel younger or look younger is laughing all the way to the bank!

Because Cheryl became aware of her new need, to look younger, her old cream no longer satisfied her need. She instantly had an expectation that it should, and it definitely wasn't promising that it would either. So her ability to trust her old cream—that is, her ability to rely on it to make her look younger—was under question. Her trust in the old cream may have looked like this:

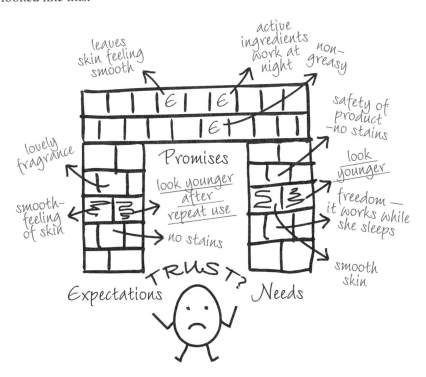

Because the new cream was promising to do what she now realized she needed, and it sounded like it was going to meet her expectations, her trust in the new cream may have looked like this:

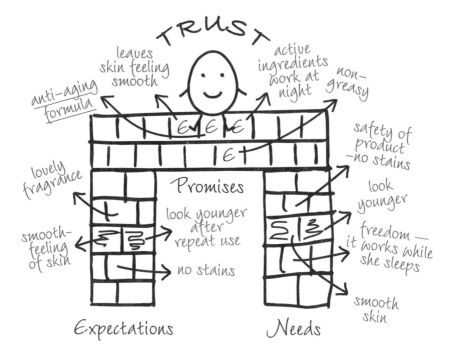

Importantly, where there is a viable alternative that promises to meet a new need, many people will switch. We touched on this earlier when we were looking at trust versus apathy.

From a branding and marketing perspective, every company should be:

1. Constantly seeking feedback from its customers about what they like and don't like about the products and services
2. Surveying the general consumer about their needs and expectations of the products and services the company offers
3. Continuing to innovate and find new ways to enhance either the offering, or the products and services themselves, to meet "new" needs
4. Making sure they can deliver on the promises

It is this last point I wanted to also touch on. I have seen so many examples of a silo mentality breaking down trust that I believe it is one of the greatest challenges in business today.

Here's what I mean. At one stage in my career I worked for a company that was secretly negotiating for a new billion-dollar customer. No one other than a select few knew what was going on. Senior management felt they could not tell the staff what was going on because they could not trust them and feared a leak to the market. When the news of the deal was finally made public, and champagne corks were popping, the rest of us realized what had happened.

In order to win this particular critical customer, senior managers made a whole bunch of promises about what was to be delivered—how, and in what time frames—and the customer needed to see things in action within forty-eight hours. While the few celebrated, the entire back office area, customer service, and everyone else who had a spare pair of hands literally raced home and came back with sleeping bags. We ordered pizza and worked around the clock for forty-eight hours in a feeble attempt to get everything ready for delivery.

In the end, we failed on some things. Tension rose between the sales and marketing people and the back office staff. The customer was not happy; the shine was quickly coming off the deal. All the market positioning and branding of the company as being responsive, there to meet the demanding needs of our customers, with quick turnaround times and a collaborative team, all looked like yet another bit of marketing hype.

The reality is it didn't have to end like that. Marketing hype is only "hype" while silos, secrecy, and lack of trust exists in organizations. Take everyone on the journey, and you can really do some amazing things for your customers!

ARE YOUR PRODUCTS AND SERVICES TRUSTWORTHY?

Fiona discussed how to build trust in marketing and branding from a strategic perspective and highlighted some key things you should be considering. I've taken some of those points, as well as things that we specifically look at in our ENP Review, to generate these questions.

Do this quick assessment and check your score at the end. Rate each question on the scale of 1 to 5:

1 = almost never

2 = rarely

3 = sometimes

4 = frequently

5 = almost always

Then tally your score.

Branding and Marketing ENPs®	
1. Our customers feel like they belong to something special when they use our products and/or services	1 2 3 4 5
2. We find out what our customer and potential customers need	1 2 3 4 5
3. Our brand provides simplicity – making the choice simple for customers	1 2 3 4 5
4. We recognise that our people are part of our brand	1 2 3 4 5
5. We work with Sales, Operations, Customer Service and Relationship Management to make sure our brand promises can be kept	1 2 3 4 5
6. We know why our customers trust us	1 2 3 4 5
7. We choose marketing channels and sponsors that match our brand	1 2 3 4 5
8. Our products and services meet their marketing and brand promises	1 2 3 4 5
9. We monitor our business partners to make sure they are protecting our brand	1 2 3 4 5
10. We measure the effectiveness of our marketing efforts	1 2 3 4 5
Overall score	

How did you do?

If you scored:

40–50: You are building a trustworthy brand. Well done; keep doing what you are doing.

30–39: You are on the way to building a trustworthy brand, but you might want to work on some areas where your score was lower.

20–29: You may want to revisit your marketing and branding strategy and tactics to build more trust and become more effective.

10–19: You may be finding that your branding and marketing efforts are not effective and not appreciated. You may want some support and advice to build trust quickly and improve results.

Download your FREE gift to help you build trust in your marketing and branding. Go to www.entente.com.au/US_Book_gifts and download your FREE e-book *7 Truths about Trust Every Marketer Needs to Know*. Check out the many resources and services at www.entente.com.au that can help you build trust in your marketing and branding.

Now, let's move into looking at trust in sales with David Penglase.

16

TRUST IN SALES

Every sale has five basic obstacles:
no need, no money, no hurry, no desire, no trust.
—Zig Ziglar, author, salesperson, and motivational speaker

INTRODUCING DAVID PENGLASE

I met David Penglase through my association with the Thought Leaders group. David delivered a presentation on sales and was engaging, kept things simple, and of course, talked about trust a lot!

David is widely recognized as Australia's leading expert on the ethics of selling. He is a dynamic, entertaining, and content-rich sales coach, conference keynote speaker, and sales workshop facilitator. David is the author of a range of books on selling, including *What's Ethical About Selling, The BASICS of Selling, Your Sales Success, The Essential Selling Series,* and *52 Success Habits for Sales Professionals.*

Supporting over two decades of experience in the fields of organization and people development, David has a bachelor's degree in business and human resource development and holds an MBA and a master's in professional ethics. (For more information about David, visit www.davidpenglase.com or www.salescoachcentral.com.)

INTRODUCTION

If you're in selling, you will understand better than most that the intangible glue that binds sustainable new, repeat, and referral business is TRUST.

Sure, the products we sell and the services we provide are important, as too are the communication strategies, the branding, and our own personality. All are strong contributors to our overall success in sales.

However, each of these in one way or another is adding to (or detracting from) the level of trust that potential and existing clients have and will continue to have in their relationships with those of us in sales.

So, let's start with a clear definition of what it is that we're talking about when we refer to selling, and this will allow us to delve a little deeper into how trust forms the intangible glue for long-term success in sales.

Selling is the process of building trust relationships with the aim to create reciprocal value on a continual basis.

Process is the delivery mechanism for trust relationships, reciprocal value, and continuity. For many salespeople who do not understand that selling is a process, it follows that they wonder why they have not been able to form stronger trust relationships with their clients, and why they are not able to deliver and receive reciprocal value on a continual basis.

HOW PROCESS DELIVERS TRUST

Without the process, selling and buying are left to chance. Without the process, planning and review are more difficult. Without the process, coaching and development are more difficult. Without the process, the quality of the interaction with the potential or existing client can be significantly reduced.

By understanding that selling is a process, we can start to gain insight to the time line of trust development as each step in the process is successfully completed.

But what sort of process? If you want to build high levels of trust with your potential and existing clients, and at the same time sell more than your competitors, your best process is to make sure that you don't try to sell.

Now, before you write that off as a ridiculous statement, the reality is that most people do not want to feel "sold." They don't want to feel pushed or coerced or manipulated into some kind of buying decision where they don't feel comfortable.

So, how do salespeople build trust to ensure that they help potential clients feel comfortable and confident that they are making a wise buying decision?

The answer is to follow a sales and communication process when engaging with potential and existing clients. Most important is that the sales and communication process that salespeople practice is one that they themselves also feel comfortable and confident in following.

What follows is a six-step sales and communication process that has trust as its fundamental principle.

Step One: Build Rapport and Deliver Value Early to Earn Trust

This first step in the sales process sets the platform upon which the other steps will either lead to a successful sale or to the departure of the potential or existing client. In fact, potential and existing clients have three "exit ramps" from which to choose when they feel a lack of trust or significant enough damage to existing levels of trust has occurred.

The first of these exit ramps that buyers can take is referred to as the initial contact fear. The initial contact fear is all about client expectations of what the buying experience is going to be like. You see, quite often, whether we like it or not in sales, we have to compete not only against our competitors but also against a negative stereotype about selling (and salespeople). You don't have to look far to discover that quite often current affairs news broadcasts will be uncovering and reporting on examples of pushy, manipulative, and coercive selling techniques being practiced by unethical salespeople.

So, is it any wonder that consumers start to subconsciously build up this picture in their minds that they've got to be on the defensive before they've even met the salesperson when they're considering making a purchase?

The more important the purchase to the consumer, the more this level of subconscious and quite often more conscious feelings of apprehension can become.

When they finally summon up enough confidence to go to make their purchase, this first exit ramp is always at the top of their mind, and their initial contact fear results in their inner voice saying to them, "What's this experience going to be like?" and "What's this salesperson going to try to do to me?"

If the salesperson ignores this first potential buyers exit ramp, they will quite likely lose the sale before the process even begins. They will not have been able to build sufficient rapport with the client to the extent where the client feels like they have received value early in the buying experience in some way, and can therefore trust the salesperson.

More on the other two buyers exit ramps later.

Salespeople need to understand that there are some basic and fundamental expectations—implicit and explicit—in the way that they are often expressed by the potential or existing clients.

Understanding these expectations enables the salesperson to better approach the selling and buying situation with the right type of attitude.

Attitude is so important because it is through our attitude that our thoughts, words, and actions will demonstrate on many levels to the buyer that they won't need the first buyers exit ramp, that they can trust us as salespeople and expect a positive buying experience.

Exactly what do clients implicitly and explicitly expect from a buying situation?

- They expect a quality product
- They expect a fair and competitive price
- They expect to be treated with respect
- They expect the product or service to perform its function well
- They expect that should there be any problems that they will be fixed within fair and equitable warranty and guarantee guidelines
- They expect to be told the truth
- They expect the salesperson to listen to and understand our needs
- They understand that businesses must make a profit, and that cheapest is not always best
- They expect the salesperson to be an expert in what they sell (and it helps if they believe in the product or service)
- They expect to be given appropriate time and information to make a wise choice

Buyers tune in very quickly to the attitude of salespeople. So if you're in sales, it's important for you not only to understand the buyers' expectations but also to understand what's driving your own attitude, your personal philosophy and belief about who you are, what you're selling, the company you work for, and the value you create when you sell what you sell.

Each of these beliefs and expectations is brought to the buyer-seller relationship very early in the process.

There's a big difference between someone who genuinely believes in the value they can create when they sell what the sell and asks, "May I help you?" and someone who lacks a personal belief in herself and her products and who asks the same question just because she has been told to ask it.

Trust is reduced dramatically when salespeople first meet with potential buyers and do not demonstrate this helping attitude. Slick opening lines or pressurized techniques at the start of the buying-selling process simply cause the first buyers exit ramp to appear, and more than likely clients will take it—either physically, by walking away, or emotionally, by staying to hear the salesperson's presentation but not really listening. In both cases it is likely to result in no sale.

When salespeople demonstrate their understanding of client expectations through an attitude of truly wanting to discover what it is that each potential buyer is looking for, the buyers are more likely to feel more comfortable and confident in the salesperson, feel that they can trust them, and be ready to enter into dialogue with the salesperson that will help them to make a wise buying decision.

This allows the selling process to move into the second step.

Step Two: Ask Questions That Reaffirm Mutual Purpose and Clarify Expectations, Needs, and Wants

Trust in the buyer-seller relationship is further built when we look for ways as salespeople to deliver value early. One way to do this is to ask clients questions about their specific situation so that you can help them articulate and clarify both for them and for you just what their expectations, needs, and wants are. In so doing, be more prepared to be able to help them make the best choice possible. And this just isn't about asking questions for the sake of asking questions: That can cause fractures in the trust that is being built between the salesperson and the buyer. Asking appropriate client value discovery questions builds trust. Asking questions that have the potential to patronize or confuse the client breaks trust.

Furthermore, any question that has the capacity for a client to think, "of course the answer is yes" has the capacity to damage trust. For example, asking something like, "Is quality important to you?" surely in most cases would result in the client thinking or saying "of course!" If you were to ask, "Is dealing with someone you can trust important to you?" surely the answer would be in most cases "of course."

The questions that salespeople ask of buyers demonstrate their purpose and their attitude. The questions that salespeople ask of buyers show the buyer that the salesperson is either looking just to make a sale or looking to find out what would be the best product(s) or service(s) that will result in the greatest amount of value being experienced by the client.

Trust deepens between salesperson and buyer when the salesperson can make a direct connection between value being sought by the buyer and value that can be created through the purchase of their products and services.

To effectively do this, salespeople need to have a clear understanding of what clients truly receive when they buy what the salesperson is selling. This is one of the most important questions that salespeople need to answer for themselves well before they meet with their clients. When clients buy from them, what are they really buying? In other words, what are the needs, wants, or problems they want solved that buying a product or service will satisfy for them?

The answers will vary depending on what the salesperson is selling. Maybe it's peace of mind, maybe it's safety, maybe it's a "wow" experience, or maybe it's entertainment. Whatever the answers are to this question, the list that is derived is what is referred to as a list of value units. The more value units you can stack up as a salesperson, the more you will be able to draw from that list and demonstrate true value for the client. You choose from the list based on the answers to the questions you ask of your clients that reveal to you what's most important to them.

That's why process is so important to building trust. If we build rapport, deliver value early by discovering and clarifying with the client their specific wants and needs, we can then move onto the next step in the process and show value.

Step Three: Show Value by Promising What You Can Deliver Will Achieve Client Expectations, Needs, and Wants

Whereas the "build rapport" step forms the foundation of trust, and the "ask questions" step reinforces that foundation, the "show value" step is what helps solidify trust.

Many salespeople lose sales because they try to sell capability and not value. Capability selling is telling the client about all of the features and benefits about the product or service, some of which may be of little interest to the client. The more the salesperson sells capability and not value, the more likely that cracks will start to appear in what seemed to be a good foundation of trust.

Why? Because, despite building rapport and asking questions, these salespeople haven't listened and are not showing value.

Showing value is about being able to repeat back to clients exactly what they have expressed that they are looking for and demonstrating how the product or service recommended will achieve what they're looking for.

This is about communicating with the client in the way that the clients need to have things communicated to them so that they understand. The more technically competent salespeople might be, the higher the danger that they may just talk technically and not in ways that the client will actually understand.

The same is true if a client is actually seeking to understand the technical side of a product or service and the salesperson is not being specific enough. Both of these examples just demonstrate to clients that the salesperson is not thinking about their specific situation. In other words, the salesperson is selling the way he or she likes to sell, not in the way that the client wants or needs to buy.

The key, therefore, in building trust when we are showing value is to communicate with clients in a way that makes them feel comfortable and that validates your purpose of trying to clarify and deliver value to them through the products and service that you offer.

Trust can be fractured when salespeople dismiss what they have learned from asking questions about their clients' situation and expectations and merely present all of the features of their products and services despite the fact they are not meeting client expectations.

This, again, demonstrates the "process" of selling.

If we've asked questions of our clients and discovered the value they seek, then delivering on that value becomes easier to explain. However, so many salespeople fail to ask appropriate questions and therefore end up only presenting product and service capability. This leaves the potential buyer to try to decipher from all the information whether what is being presented will actually create the value he or she is expecting.

For salespeople to stay "true" to the process of building trust, step four enables reassurance and clarity to occur for both salesperson and buyer.

Step Four: Identify Obstacles That Could Potentially Be Barriers to Reciprocal Value Being Experienced

The key to ensuring that salespeople do not damage trust through inappropriate presentation of their products and services or "capability dumping" is to seek feedback from the buyer. The feedback you want is whether the salesperson is explaining and demonstrating the information the client is seeking and in ways that demonstrate how their expectations of the product or service will be delivered.

Rather than rambling on about all of the features, benefits, and value that can be created by the products and services, it is important for salespeople to regularly check whether they are covering what their client wants to know and in ways that the client understands.

This can be achieved by simple feedback and opinion questions such as:

- Am I covering the areas that are most important to you?
- Have I provided you with the information you're after?
- Does that make sense to you?
- Is there anything that I haven't covered that you'd like me to go over?

When asked with genuine interest and care, feedback and opinion questions demonstrate to customers that sales staff have their best interests in mind. These types of questions help the client and the salesperson clarify and articulate the real needs and wants of the client. This helps to ensure that the discussion around the features and benefits of the product or service is demonstrating the true value that is most important to the client.

When this is done with a true purpose and attitude of wanting to do their job properly, salespeople add further strength to the trust building between themselves and their potential and existing clients.

For this reason, if salespeople ask great questions and present value based on what they have discovered, obstacles or objections to buying are reduced. Why? Because the client is experiencing a "value-match" between what they expect and what is being presented. This makes the next step in a sales process merely a confirmation and not what is typically regarded as a strategic and technique-based stage in a sale.

Step Five: Confirm the Sale by Explaining the Next Appropriate Actions for Reciprocal Value to Be Exchanged

In traditional selling approaches, the "close" is a process of steering the client to make a decision and then asking for a buying decision by using one or more of a series of closing techniques. Typically, those techniques have included the puppy-dog close; the hat-in-hand close; the either-or close; and the slip up on them when they're not looking and kick them in the kidney close—all of which most salespeople don't feel good about trying and certainly cause the second buyers exit ramp to appear in front of the client.

The second buyers exit ramp appears to clients when they actually like what is being presented by the salesperson, but they are pushed a little too hard to make a buying decision before they are ready. The voice inside their head says something like, "This sounds good, but if I say yes, what risk might I run...what might go wrong?"

Trust is damaged when salespeople push too hard for a sale.

However, successful salespeople aim not just to win a sale, they aim to do so in ways that encourage clients to want to buy repeatedly from them and/or to refer others to them.

Successful salespeople understand that when they have clarified what the client is after and have demonstrated clearly how what they are offering will deliver on that value, asking for a decision to buy should not cause any pressure or stress on either the salesperson or the buyer.

Successful salespeople are confident and comfortable with simply asking the client—proactively, but not pushing them—something like, "Based on what we've covered, is there anything else you need to know or that I could help you with before we proceed?"

When clients can see that the salesperson believes in the value his or her product can create, and that they are not being pushed into making a buying decision, they will feel more comfortable and confident about making the buying decision. This is the essence of trust in the sale and buying process.

For salespeople to build their comfort and confidence in asking clients for buying decisions, they can apply a "light of day test" to their sales process and purpose. The light of day test is simply this: If the person they are selling to was a family member or a dear friend, would they sell what they are selling in the way that they are selling it? If the answer is yes, then the salesperson should be very comfortable and have every confidence in asking the client for a buying decision.

However, if they would feel uncomfortable about selling what they are selling in the way that they are selling it, then perhaps something needs to change in their process to help them engage and build trust and to earn the right to receive a positive answer when asking clients for a buying decision.

However, what truly cements trust in a buying and selling situation is not what happens during the sale, it's what happens after the sale.

Step Six: Stay in Touch to Deliver on Promises, to Thank the Client, and to Demonstrate Reciprocal Value on a Continual Basis

So far in this discussion we have been focusing on the first two elements of our definition of selling. They are that selling is a process and that the process, when completed with a client-focused and value-centric purpose, will build trust relationships.

Our sixth step in the selling process introduces us to the third and fourth key elements of the definition of selling, which are the aim to create reciprocal value and to do so on a continual basis.

Salespeople get the business they deserve and they get the referrals they deserve. The level of new, repeat, and referral business is usually based on not just the buying experience but also the post-purchase validation that the client receives (or not).

When clients refer their friends, family, and colleagues to salespeople, they are putting their personal integrity on the line. They are saying that I trust this salesperson and that's why I am referring you to them. These "warm referrals" from our existing clients fast-track the sales process by helping to overcome the first buyers exit ramp (the initial contact fear).

The referred potential client is entering the buying situation with a transferred level of trust: transferred from the person who referred them, which is also known as referred trust. In order for our existing clients to feel confident and comfortable enough to refer their friends, family, and colleagues, we must create an environment of trust in promising what we can deliver and delivering on what we promise. This is all about managing the third buyers exit ramp.

The third buyers exit ramp occurs after the sale. It is known as the post-sale fear. The client has made their purchase, he gets home or back to his office, and thinks to himself, "What have I just done? Was it a good decision?" And in many cases, because such people never receive any further contact from the salesperson or any further validation of their purchasing decision, this post-sale fear can lead to a "validation void" which reduces the value and pleasure that the client can potentially receive from an important purchase.

When salespeople find ways to "thank" the client and to demonstrate after the sale that they value the client's business, the level of trust that is built becomes significant and leads to advocacy: that is, clients who are comfortable and prepared to tell others about the value they've received and readily refer them to the salespeople who have delivered that value.

This might be a simple phone call after the sale to check on delivery and to ensure that the client is happy with what was received. It might be a card of thanks in the mail. It could be an additional "gift" of some kind that will help clients enjoy their purchase even more. Whatever it is, by sending loud and clear messages to clients that the salesperson was not just after a sale, but that she truly wanted to present and deliver on the client's expectations, needs, and wants, has a significant and long-term impact on the level of trust that the client has with that salesperson and future purchasing decisions.

Put simply, this final step in the sales process is a validation that the salesperson has promised what he could deliver and he has delivered on his promises.

You don't *get* trust; you *earn* trust. And trust is earned in sales by first

- Understanding what the client's expectations are
- Understanding what they're looking for in making a purchase
- Finding out how they like to go about making those purchasing decisions

It's this final point that's worth considering. How do clients like to go about making their purchasing decisions?

THE SAMENESS SYNDROME

Quite often, the choice between one product and a competitive product is not sufficiently differentiated by the price. And when faced with a choice between one product and a competitive product, the client likewise often realizes that either product will meet their needs and/or wants; there is a "sameness" about the products. The buyer, then, will typically make a purchase decision based on a hierarchy of deciding values. For that reason, salespeople can build even deeper levels of trust with clients when they can "tap into" each client's dominant deciding values.

The first dominant deciding value is "Ease." Some customers will buy one product over another because the salesperson was able to put them at ease and reduce or remove any level of apprehension about the purchase by demonstrating the track record, quality, or warranty of the product.

The second dominant deciding value is "Ego." Some customers will buy one product over another because the salesperson made the buyer feel special and important, or they might choose to buy the product because of a strong association with the brand and image that the brand represents.

The third dominant deciding value is "Enjoyment." Some customers will buy one product over another because the salesperson made the buying experience fun and an enjoyable experience.

The fourth dominant deciding value is "Evidence." Some customers will buy one product over another because the salesperson proves and provides evidence that the product will do what the client wants and needs it to do.

So, the dominant deciding values are linked to but distinct from the actual needs of the client.

Trust can be fractured in the buying-selling process when the salesperson understands the wants and needs of the client, but he or she presents products or services without understanding that client's dominant deciding values. For example, if the salesperson is focusing on a product's track record, quality, or warranty but the client first and foremost just wants a fun buying experience, the client may not feel as "connected" with the salesperson and may choose to do business with someone else.

Another example that demonstrates that people buy for different reasons is the purchase of the same make and model of a car. One customer is buying the car because of the image and ego. Another is buying because of the proven safety, reliability, and demonstrated track record. Another is buying because it comes in the color he wants. Yet another is buying because of the economical fuel consumption.

People buy for different reasons, and what they look for in most purchasing situations (consciously or subconsciously) are salespeople who are tuned into not just what they as customers are after, but more specifically their fundamental needs and reasons as to why they want to make the purchase.

Arguably, anyone can sell anything once and maybe get away with it. However, salespeople who approach the sale as a process of building trust relationships with the aim to create reciprocal value on a continual basis will, in the long run, far outsell those who are just looking for the quick sale or the "doable deal."

David has raised a couple of issues that might need to be clarified in the context of the earlier chapters in the book.

One was his comment about implicit and explicit expectations. I wondered whether I should have included that in the trust model. We talk about implicit and explicit promises, as you know, but there are implicit and explicit expectations—and needs, for that matter.

The reason I chose not to complicate the model is purely that I believe we should be asking people what they expect and need in any case. Some people will openly tell you some (these expectations and needs become explicit), and not tell you others, but they behave in a way that may demonstrate what those expectations and needs are (therefore they may remain implicit).

The important thing in building trust is to uncover as many expectations and needs as you can. The more that exist that you are unaware of, the more likely it is that trust is inadvertently breaking down if there is any form of reliance on you to deliver an outcome.

I'll give you an example, drawing on David's example of reasons why people buy cars.

Peter has always loved Mercedes Benz automobiles. As he walked into the company's showroom, a young salesman came up and shook his hand. "Can I help you, or are you just looking at this stage?" he asked.

"No, you can probably help me. I'm interested in getting back into a Benz. I've always loved them even though I defected for a while. I think I know which model I'm after." Peter said as he walked over to the particular model.

The salesman's eyes widened. "I love this car. It has so many more features than the previous models. Let me show you." He proceeded to push buttons and point out all the features that were different or enhanced.

Peter said to him, "I'd just like to take it for a test drive, if that's OK, but I'm pretty much sold. It's just a matter of choosing colors and then what you can give me on a trade in."

They took the car out for a drive, and as they came back into the showroom, the salesman said, "Do you want to take a look under the hood?"

"No. Not really. I don't even think I'd recognize anything anymore."

"Oh, come on. I just love these cars. I could talk about them all day," said the salesman. He popped the hood and Peter had a quick look.

When they finally went in to work out the figures, the salesman said he would need to get back to Peter with a trade-in price on his other car.

"OK. That's fine. I'll tell you what I'm after color wise and you can see if there's a car in stock."

They determined that the salesman would have to make some phone calls and would get back to Peter the following day. A week later, a postcard arrived from the salesman saying, "Dear Peter. Thanks for your visit to our showroom. If there is anything we can do for you, please give me a call," and it was signed by the salesman.

Sadly, this is actually a true story. Not surprisingly, Peter bought a different car from a different dealer!

Peter's dominant deciding value was Ease, but the salesman was treating him as if his dominant value was Evidence. He had a basic need that was explicit: to buy that particular model of car as soon as the figures were worked out. His dominant deciding value of Ease was directly linked to his need.

Peter also had an implicit expectation that he could walk in and do a deal. Why? Because he had done that before. Why was it implicit? Because he didn't come out and state it, but we rarely do state our expectations. In this case, the role of the salesman was to find out exactly what Peter expected and needed, and how he wanted to buy. Instead, he lost the sale by not meeting Peter's expectations or needs.

One other thing David mentioned was "expectations, needs, and wants." A few people have asked me where "wants" sit on the Trust Model. As far as my ability to trust is concerned, what I "want" does not come into the picture unless it becomes an expectation or a need. I may "want" a huge bunch of flowers from my partner, but if I do not expect it, and I don't need it, and it has not been promised to me, then my ability to trust my partner has no connection to whether I receive a bunch of flowers from him or not. If I did (and I do, incidentally), it would be a surprise, and may then become an expectation in the future.

From purely a sales perspective, a salesperson absolutely needs to uncover wants, because this helps him or her determine the value of the product or service to the buyer. If the buyer realizes that the want can actually be realized, it may become a need and an expectation, and may now also be promised, throwing it instantly into the trust wall.

ARE YOU A TRUSTWORTHY SALESPERSON?

David gave some great insights into building trust in the sales process, including things all salespeople should be doing. I've taken some of those points, as well as the Trustworthy Person Model and have created some questions for people who are selling products and services.

Do this quick assessment and check your score at the end. Rate each question on the scale of 1 to 5:

1 = almost never

2 = rarely

3 = sometimes

4 = frequently

5 = almost always

Then tally your score.

Openness and Transparency	
I am open to ideas and suggestions on new, improved ways to 'sell' our products and services	1 2 3 4 5
I share information about myself with potential customers when talking with them	1 2 3 4 5
Score (Total of both questions)	

Honesty and with Integrity	
I am honest about our products and services when talking with potential customers	1 2 3 4 5
I treat my potential customers and customers fairly and with respect	1 2 3 4 5
Score (Total of both questions)	

Genuine and Authentic	
As a salesperson I am true to my core beliefs and values	1 2 3 4 5
If I was asked to compromise my core values and beliefs I would challenge that rather than go along with it	1 2 3 4 5
Score (Total of both questions)	

Courageous and Decisive	
I am confident in approaching potential customers	1 2 3 4 5
I admit when I've made a mistake	1 2 3 4 5
Score (Total of both questions)	

Reliable and Proven	
I only promise what I know I can deliver	1 2 3 4 5
I manage people's expectations of me as a salesperson	1 2 3 4 5
Score (Total of both questions)	

Caring and Empathetic	
I take time to understand the expectations and needs of potential customers	1 2 3 4 5
I consider how potential customers might be feeling	1 2 3 4 5
Score (Total of each question)	
Overall score	

How did you do?

If you scored:

48–60: You are building trustworthy relationships and should be seeing the rewards of that. Well done.

36–47: You are doing OK, but have a few areas to work on to be more effective. Take note and make some changes to your sales technique.

24–35: You may be finding that you are not as effective as you'd like to be in your sales role. You need to build more trusted relationships. Take note of the areas in which you had a lower score, and create an action plan—today!

12–23: You may be struggling in your role as a salesperson and should ask your immediate superior for support or coaching to build trust and improve your effectiveness in your sales approach. Do so immediately.

Download your FREE gift to help you build trust in your sales process. Go to www.entente.com.au/US_Book_gifts and download your FREE e-book *7 Truths about Trust Every Salesperson Needs to Know*. Check out the many resources and services at www.entente.com.au that can help you build trust in your sales process.

Now let's move on to look at trust in customer service with Iven Frangi.

17

TRUST IN
CUSTOMER SERVICE

The key to longevity is to keep doing what you do better than anyone else.
We work real hard at that. It's about getting your message out to the consumer.
It's about getting their trust, but also getting them excited, again and again.
—Ralph Lauren, fashion designer and businessman

INTRODUCING IVEN FRANGI

I met Iven at a (you guessed it) Thought Leaders event! Iven is *the* man when it comes to presentations, especially on how to create and deliver incredible customer experiences.

Iven's studied marketing. In sales he has been a qualifying member of the "Million Dollar Round Table," and as the youngest regional manager at Australia's fastest growing life insurance company, he supervised more than fifty branches and a team with production in excess of $13 million annually.

Iven thoroughly researches each client's needs and environment to design presentations that create impact. He adds value to his work by weaving in real-life examples, humor, and activities to engage the audience in the process.

Since 1991 Iven has been making presentations ranging from keynotes to customized workshops. He is a contributor to the number-one best seller *Body Language* by Allan Pease. He is a past board member of the National Speakers Association. Iven is fascinated with people and the way they interact and do business, and he is able to give his clients ideas and skills they can immediately put into practice—profitably. (To find out more about Iven, visit his website at www.frangi.com.)

MOMENTS OF TRUST: HOW TO MAKE YOUR BUSINESS A CUSTOMER MAGNET

You can talk about trust as much as you want. You can theorize about what trust is and isn't. In business, however, if your customers don't trust you, you have a serious problem. It's all about the customer experience.

In his book *Moments of Truth,* author Jan Carlzon put forward what we now see as an established business premise: Every time a customer interacts with your business, in that moment they discover the true character of the business. Is the business able to deliver on the promises that are made in advertising and branding messages? Carlson argues that this was the moment that truth was discovered.

I believe this is a moment of trust. I believe that trust is a more valuable moment than one of truth. Why? Because the discovery you make in your moment of truth is whether or not you have validated that you can trust the business or person with whom you are interacting.

Every time a customer interacts with your business, no matter what the touch point, that person has an experience. The question for the business is this: Was the experience that was delivered the one that we wanted to deliver or the one that the customer ended up with? The customer's experience is the tangible demonstration of the level of trust he has in the person with whom he did business.

In the balance of this chapter I will explain why customer experience management is the core of a business's trust proposition and what you, the reader, can do to make your business magnetic to customers.

Trust Is Tangible

The Entente Trust Model is an excellent tool to use when evaluating the way trust is created. The blend of our expectations and needs and the promises made succinctly describes what happens when we evaluate trust. The thing is, customers do this with our products and services every day.

A simple expectation a customer has about the way she will be treated when she walks into your branch, the need to be able to easily find something on a shelf so he gets in and out of your store quickly, the promise of reliable delivery of a product within forty-eight hours—each one, if not met, results in a breakdown of trust.

While many people think that trust is a "fluffy" thing that cannot be measured, the reality is that two consequential factors are present in every business. They are hard and soft differentiators.

A hard differentiator is anything that can be measured, counted, or calculated. Examples include, among others, delivery on time, quality of a product, or performance. A soft differentiator is anything that has to be evaluated, weighed, or estimated. This would include honesty in dealings, performance (this is both hard and soft), and, of course, trust.

Trust is always a combination of hard and soft differentiators, and in every interaction we have with a business, we encounter both differentiators. Naturally, hard differentiators are easier to keep track of. Soft differentiators are felt rather than calculated and, in most cases, have a larger impact than do hard differentiators.

MAGNETIC CUSTOMER XPERIENCES

The way we track how we feel about a product or service or a business is by keeping an internal score. The overall description of what we feel is our experience. Leading businesses today are realizing that managing the customer's experience is a critical part of building their business.

This is a model that explains what needs to be taken into account when managing customer experience. Until recently, customer relationship management and customer service have been the predominant tools in the kit of strategies to build customer growth. Others include customer loyalty and customer satisfaction.

Customer experience management is the next business imperative. It provides the framework and architecture that leverages all of these tools to create an experience that attracts and retains customers. Most businesses gather information so they can get to know their customers. Customer experience management flips this and focuses, instead, on what your customer can learn about you and your business.

Trust Is an Outcome of Expectations

Before we do business with a person or a company, we have some expectations about what's going to happen. Sometimes what we expect is clear and well defined. For example, taking a flight. If we choose a budget airline like Virgin Blue, we expect that they will get us to where we are going with a no-frills approach. You buy your own food and drink, manage your own carry-on luggage, and know that seating is first come first served (all hard differentiators of the product or service). One size fits all, and if price is significant then the trade-off is all about what the airline doesn't do as much as what it does.

If we book Qantas, things are a little different. Our expectations will vary depending on where we are seated on the aircraft. This was explained to me by Keith Yates, the CEO and founder of Performa, a company that specializes in designing experiences for airline passengers and prestige brands. I sat next to Keith on a flight. He explained that the customer experience varies as you move down the aisle.

In first class the differentiators are many. The hard ones include wider seats that fold down to become flat beds, gourmet food, movies on demand, staff who put your luggage in the storage area for you. The soft differentiators may include the courtesy and friendliness of the staff, the lack of urgency in the meal service, the reduced noise in the cabin from other passengers, but prestige and status are the central soft differentiators.

Trust here is on steroids and is therefore often more fragile. With a rise in cost comes a rise in expectations. "I trust that, because I have paid you all this extra money, you will truly make this experience worth it."

As we proceed down the aisle, we pass the business class passengers, who have many of the same expectations as those in first class. We eventually reach the back, filled with the infrequent flyers and vacationers. They want a meal, a seat, and an opportunity to have some fun. Their moment of trust revolves around what is most significant to them: the opportunity to get away at a reasonable price. They are unlikely to become advocates for the in-flight service or comfort of the seats like those at the pointy end. They may, however, recommend the airline based on timely arrival and the quality in-flight movies.

I work with my clients to migrate customers from being people who use their products to being advocates who brag about them. We do this by creating a Magnetic Customer Xperience (see the illustration that follows). Magnetic Xperiences are not an accident, they don't happen by chance. Rather, they are planned, predictable, and profitable. Trust is at the core of creating and sustaining a Magnetic Customer Xperience. The reason for this is that trust is the glue that binds the customer to a business and also makes the relationship malleable. *Trust creates magnetism.*

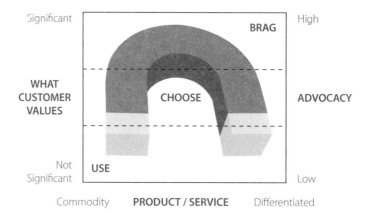

Magnetic Customer Experiences

Any relationship, business or personal, needs trust in order to survive. Without trust, the relationship is brittle. Apply pressure to something that is brittle and it will break. Trust supplies the flexibility so that when pressure is applied, the relationship flexes and bends to accommodate challenge and change.

This fits with the Magnetic Customer Xperience model's three influences.

- Differentiation. This looks at whether or not the product or service is a commodity or highly differentiated. The differentiators can be hard or soft. The more highly differentiated a product is, the more it stands out.
- Significance. This refers to the importance or meaning the product or service has to a customer. The greater the degree of significance, the greater the level of trust that needs to exist. For our airline passengers the significance could range from prestige to in-flight movies.
- Advocacy. This is a calculation of the number of people who will brag about your business. There are various ways of calculating this. Satisfaction is a dead measure: You can have highly satisfied customers even as your business is going broke. The most popular form of measuring advocacy is the Net Promoter Score, or simply

NPS, developed by Harvard alumnus Fred Reichheld. (For more details, see his book *The Ultimate Question: Driving Good Profits and True Growth* [Harvard Business School Press, 2006].) The customer is asked a single question: "How likely is it that you would recommend this company to a friend or colleague?" Each customer's answer is scored by taking the net result of promoters and detractors and expressing that as a positive or a negative number. A positive score means the business has more promoters than detractors.

As the levels of differentiation and significance grow, we move from being just users of a product to using the product or service as a deliberate choice. If we reach the highest levels of significance, and what we are using is highly differentiated, then we are going to brag to others. It's impossible to achieve high levels of advocacy without high levels of trust. Why? Because customers do not brag about an experience where they did not get what they were promised, or what they expected or needed. They nag about the negative experience. Broken trust creates detractors for your business.

Our Level of Trust Is Determined by Either Makers or Breakers

Makers and breakers that affect your customers are the biggest factors that will impact your long-term success. How you manage them will make or break your business.

A maker is something a business does that enhances and reinforces a magnetic experience. A breaker is the opposite. It damages the experience and pushes people away from your business. Makers and breakers are the biggest determinant of your trust quotient because they support or destroy the expectations people have about your business.

Next time you listen to someone or read something about a product or service, notice what he or she is really concerned with. People will describe what they like or dislike about what they have experienced. For example:

"It looks great."

"When I got the thing home, I couldn't get it to work."

"The people were really helpful."

"I phoned them and got put through to the wrong department."

"They promised to have it ready today, and now they are saying next Tuesday."

What we talk about and illustrate is the experience we had. That's what your customers do and what your potential customers get as feedback. What you and I describe and hear is what we consider to be the makers and breakers. We are defining and describing moments of trust.

Makers and Breakers Come in Various Shapes, Sizes, and Levels of Impact Here is an exercise you can do to evaluate your business makers and breakers.

1. Look at your business and make a list of the makers and breakers.
2. Decide the size and impact of each entry on each list and how they affect the advocacy score for your business.
3. Determine what breakers could be makers and what effect the switch would have.
4. Establish what the effect of the new offerings would be on the customers.
5. Implement the makers, remove the breakers, and evaluate the outcome.
6. Start the process again at item one to see what else can be done.

You could even do this exercise with some of your customers. They may well have a different perception of your makers and breakers than you do.

Makers and Breakers in Action = Trust Outcome Let's look at some specific examples of how to move a breaker into the maker category.

Breaker: There is a lot of focus on frequent flyer miles and how many you get from airlines and credit cards. But have you ever tried to actually use the points you've accumulated? At any gathering of people who travel, for business or pleasure, ask about cashing in these points and stand back. You will hear a discussion of trust in the promised outcome.

Size = Huge
Impact on NPS = Detractor
Outcome = Trust damaged

Maker: Virgin Blue came out with an "any seat on any flight" program. It fits their brand and the "up the establishment" ethos.

Size = Substantial
Impact on NPS = Promoter
Outcome = Trust restored over other brands

Breaker: Moving to another location has many potential breakers. One really is a "breaker": The movers can literally break your furniture. So you buy insurance, which is a moneymaker for the movers and mostly resented by customers who feel ripped off at having to insure against a "supplier at fault" problem.

Size = Depends on the value can be very large
Impact on NPS = Detractor
Outcome = Reinforces our negative trust belief

Maker: Any organization that offers a genuine guarantee such as "If we damage it, we will fix it." This provides a great opportunity to turn a breaker into a maker. What's your trust guarantee?

Size = Huge
Impact on NPS = Promoter
Outcome = Building trust

BUILD TRUST OR BUILD AN EXIT STRATEGY

Let's have a look at what's happening in the market with regard to customers and what they are doing and demanding. The major shift is the transfer of commercial power from the manufacturer/seller to the customer.

Ten years ago the manufacturer/seller of a product determined what the customer knew and understood about what was being offered. We read brochures and listened to the salespeople to gather information. We also listened to our friends to balance what the manufacturer/seller let us know. What our friends told us influenced our decisions.

Now we take notice of many more sources of information and opinions. It is estimated that 67 percent of people Google information before making a major purchase. Accepting what the manufacturer/seller says as the only or the major source of information is a thing of the past.

The Internet has had a major impact on how we, as customers, establish and change our expectations about what we can get and from what source. Forums, chat rooms, and consumer sites abound. Pick up a business, a special interest, or an in-flight magazine, and they all have a product evaluation section with comments on how products and services perform—or don't. Add to this the expanding number of Web sites devoted to product evaluation (for example, versiontracker.com and znet.com), and the choices we have become broader and potentially more confusing.

This is the shift from product and service centric to customer centric. Customers now have information that shapes their decisions and, because the information comes from multiple sources, trust becomes a central issue. Who and what we trust is also part of the shift. Now we have to evaluate the motives of any source of information for any hidden agendas, such as advertorial, product promotion, product placement, sponsorship, subsidiary company, and political or interest group bias.

As our information sources widen, what we question is the depth of the opinion expressed. There is also a domino effect: If we trust the original source of our information, then we are more likely to trust the places to which they refer us. Often our evaluation filters recede as we move to people, places, and businesses that we've been referred to or are recommended. The more we trust the source, the more we trust the referral or recommendation.

In 2005, having conducted their seventh annual trust survey, Edelman found that 45 percent of people surveyed said their most trusted information source was personal contacts, with only 4 percent trusting advertisements. (Excerpted from a presentation titled "Stakeholder Expectations of Corporate Asia.")

CUSTOMERS DEMONSTRATE THEIR TRUST, AND BUSINESS IS USING THAT KNOWLEDGE

The power shift is also being reflected in the new terms used by, and behavioral practices of, consumers, because behavior is one of the most reliable indicators of trust.

"Tryvertising," "insperience," and "customer made" (which I'll explain in detail in the next section) are terms coined by TrendWatch ("the collective postings of some of the FullSIX Group's designers, strategists, and consultants on new media and marketing trends"). Both these terms and their practice are on the rise and further point to how the pattern of trust is shifting. Tryvertising is where we are given the opportunity to try products before buying them. This is the trust-building response of some smart businesses to the need for consumers to feel more comfortable before they make a purchase. Ikea pioneered this idea. One of the major reasons for their worldwide success is the original design of their stores, which allows everything on sale to be examined, sat on, opened, laid down on, stood on, and thoroughly examined.

Cingular (now AT&T Wireless) is an example of a cell phone company following the age-old practice of car dealers by having showrooms outfitted with all the latest products. The target market gets to play with them so they get excited and buy them.

Tryvertising is a trust strategy. Before you buy, be comfortable, know exactly what to expect, become familiar with something you may never have seen before. Know how a new product meets your needs, and that what the manufacturer/seller says it does, it actually delivers on.

Tryvertising describes what a product does. So does insperience. It's about building trust by allowing a customer to experience a product or service. The difference between the two is in their names. Trying is sampling; an insperience is immersion.

Let's say you want to get fitter, and you are contemplating hiring a personal trainer. An insperience would be built around the trainer scheduling you for the first session and giving you an opportunity to experience the dynamic of the relationship. Tryvertising might be having a group of personal trainers at an event where you could talk to them about what they do, and they could walk you through what a training program might look like for you.

On a larger scale, insperiences are about you and me wanting to reproduce what we experience in the retail and business world and bringing those experiences back to our private or domestic domains. One of the notable examples is going to the movies. We love the whole immersion in the dark, surround sound, free-of-diversion environment in a movie theater.

In the United States, the National Association of Home Builders says that 36 percent of people building new homes want a media room, with the majority spending anywhere from $5,000 to $55,000 on their systems. (Details are available on their Web site, at www.nahb.org.) These people go into stores and sit in a room furnished with the recliner chairs, huge screens, curtains, and projection systems. All the surroundings can be transplanted into their homes.

The Australian leader in this industry is entertainment icon Barry Bull of Toombul music. (For more details, visit www.toombulmusic.com.au.) Barry has gone one stage further to create the "intelligent home": a fully integrated system that controls key electrical appliances and services and allows them to be controlled remotely. From a trust perspective this takes the guesswork out of getting it right yourself. It's highly significant, and it makes your home (your personal domestic brand) highly differentiated.

TO GET CONTROL, LET GO

"Let go of control. Let go of deciding the direction your products and services will take. Just stand back and let your customers decide what will happen next. Hand over control to the Global Brain."

That's the mantra of the businesses on the cutting edge of Customer Xperience Management. They are relinquishing control of deciding what happens next. No, they aren't giving away managing the business. What they are saying is that if you really, truly want to have a genuine customer-centric business, then you have to put your customers at the center of what is happening. This could be the ultimate trust strategy.

This innovation is called "customer made." TrendWatch defines this as, "The phenomenon of corporations creating goods, services, and experiences in close cooperation with experienced and creative consumers, tapping into their intellectual capital, and in exchange giving them a direct say in (and rewarding them for) what actually gets produced, manufactured, developed, designed, serviced, or processed."

Businesses that have embarked on the customer-made path have not lost their minds. They have simply decided that the so-called Global Brain may be better than theirs. They have also realized that their existing and would-be customers already possess the ideas, information, and feedback about their business that could rocket them forward if they could effectively tap into that knowledge.

We have all had this experience. We have just bought, or attempted to buy, a product or service and have been frustrated when for some reason— no stock, poor answers, a hard-to-navigate Web site, unhelpful staff—it couldn't be done. So we think to ourselves, "If somebody would just ask me, I know exactly what they need to do to fix this business!"

Customer made is not just a feedback device that asks for opinions with no real answers. It's not customization; it's not just window dressing to look like you care. It is a real strategy to deliver what is desired. You could even find out what your customers would most want to buy from you next. It's a real and tangible way of co-creating the way your business moves forward. Co-creating with your customers the experience or Xperience they really, truly want, expect, and need.

Just who is doing it, making it work?

Magnetic Customer Xperiences are built on the fact that a magnet has two poles: positive and negative. Xperience builders know that their job is to enhance or accentuate the positive elements of a business and reduce or eliminate the negative aspects of what is delivered. Creating Magnetic Xperiences on your own can be difficult. You may be guessing, and if you're guessing, you could be getting it wrong! Instead, tap into the Global Brain.

For instance, British-based mobile network operator Vodafone released a TV ad that was the result of a design competition, which they advertised worldwide. And what innovative product would Nokia next create? They created a "Concept Lounge" in 2005 in Benelux for the next cool phone design. The Global-Brain competition brought forward a Turkish designer named Tamer Nakisci. His innovative idea is the "Nokia 888." (More details can be found at http://nokia-insider.com/news/2006/1/30/nokia-888.)

Closer to home in Australia, there's Liam Mulhall at Brewtopia. His team brought a concept for a new beer to life via the Internet (truly a Global Brain), where everything was designed including the bottle and the style of the brew. Truly customer made: You get to design your own labels and have it home-delivered. Did it work? After four years of development, the company was listed on the stock exchange. You can now get your own branded wine or water as well. Accentuate the positive? Brewtopia even got American celebrity David "The Hoff" Hasselhoff to endorse, or rather comment, on the brew. (Check it out at www.brewtopia.com.au.)

Global giant Procter & Gamble uses the Global Brain to make dealing with them more magnetic. Its connect-and-develop program and other projects now contribute more than 35 percent of the company's innovations. In fact, research and development productivity at Procter & Gamble has increased by nearly 60 percent. In the past two years, the company has launched more than 100 new products for which some aspect of development came from outside the company. According to the March 2006 issue of the *Harvard Business Review,* Procter & Gamble's most successful connect-and-develop products to hit the market are Olay Regenerist, Swiffer Dusters, the Crest SpinBrush, and the Mr. Clean Magic Eraser. (Still more details are available at www.pg.com.)

What can you do? Creating Magnetic Xperiences is about talking to our customers, potential customers, and even those who are not customers who may have ideas to contribute. The combination of feedback and innovation can drive your business forward faster than you may be able to do it by yourself or with just your own staff.

By accentuating the positives and eliminating the negatives using the Global Brain and the insights and opinions of your customers, you will not only create new, innovative products and services your customers can trust but also know which products and services to get rid of—the ones your customers no longer trust because they no longer meet their ever-changing needs.

START A CUSTOMER CONVERSATION

There is a range of technologies you could use to start and manage a meaningful customer conversation. Trust is created in two-way conversations. Your customers will willingly co-create a better business than you have now. They have a vested interest in doing it! Your customers will tell you which parts of the customer experience are negative—which you should reduce or eliminate—and which ones are positive—which you should extend or accentuate. Your customers are already telling someone about what you are doing. Are you capturing their feedback?

When you build a business with your customers' input, two things happen. First, when your focus is on the customer and what to do to demonstrate that you are trustworthy, the entire energy of your business will shift. Your business will become magnetic; your customers will know you can be trusted, and they will brag about you.

Second, if you give people an experience they can't get anywhere else, they won't go anywhere else. Jan Carlzon's great book, *Moments of Truth* (Ballinger Publishing Co., 1987), and its truths are still vital. I believe that moments of truth give customers an understanding of one other, more important factor. In a moment of truth you are evaluating whether you can trust the business. The business that wants to be truly magnetic will value a customer's trust more highly than they value the money from the next sale.

If you would like to evaluate your business, go to www.cxm.com.au and click on the free Magnetic Xperience Evaluator in the left margin.

Iven has raised a few points that I thought I'd like to elaborate on here.

The first one is the concept of hard and soft differentiators. Iven talks about a hard differentiator as being "anything that can be measured, counted, or calculated." The study he referred to looked at delivery on time, quality, or performance. A soft differentiator was defined as "anything that has to be evaluated, weighed, or estimated." Why is trust always a combination of both hard and soft differentiators, and what does this mean for businesses?

As we know, the promises that are made by businesses can be around such hard things as when products will be delivered, how something will work, what something will do for you in real, tangible terms. But promises, especially implicit ones, are often made by businesses around the "soft" things, like how a product will make you feel, how you might be perceived by others if you have a certain product, and how "valuable" a product or service can be to you.

The hard differentiators, the explicit promises, can usually be measured. You can tell whether the goods were delivered on time or not; your customers will tell you even if you don't figure it out for yourself. The soft differentiators, the implicit promises, are those instances when customers connect on an emotional level with your product or service. They experience what you have to offer in a very personal way, and in a way that may vary from customer to customer. How on earth do you measure that, and how do you keep delivering on that?

This is where the Global Brain concept, the customer-made concept, comes in. The more you involve your customers in the process of innovation and product development, the more you will know what they value and what they expect and need from their interaction with you and your products and services, and the more you can create ways to turn some of those soft differentiators into hard measurable ones.

Another subject Iven talked about is advocacy: having your customers brag about you. He draws a distinction between customer satisfaction and advocacy that is interesting, and something I have picked up on in my research too. Can you have satisfied customers while going broke? What is the difference between satisfied customers and customers who are advocates and bragging?

My mother has her little "brag books" at home. (Of course, this is to satisfy those people who do not have digital photos on their computer!) A brag book is a little photo album that gets carried around and pulled out at any opportunity to show friends, people at functions, the person sitting next to you on the bus—basically anyone who will listen—pictures of your children and grandchildren.

Wouldn't you just love your customers to have the equivalent of a brag book about you! Think about it. Your customers become your unpaid sales force. Now *that's* powerful. What makes people so proud that they want to share pictures of their children and grandchildren? They have made some contribution to the outcome: "I created them. They came from me. Look, they've got my eyes." People certainly don't show pictures of their neighbors' children in the same way.

If you involve your customers in the creation of your products and services, they can have some sense of having helped create them, and they will brag about them. Input into the creation of products and services can secure the reliability of them meeting expectations and needs, as well as keeping their promises, which is why customers can brag and not nag, and why they trust in the outcome.

True advocates for your business will drive more business to you; this is where the difference between satisfied customers and advocates lies.

DO YOUR CUSTOMERS TRUST YOU?

Iven shared some great information about building trust to enhance the customer "Xperience." I've taken some of those points and considered some ENPs to create the following questions for you to consider as you explore how you are building trust with your customers.

Do this quick assessment and check your score at the end. Rate each question on the scale of 1 to 5:

1 = almost never

2 = rarely

3 = sometimes

4 = frequently

5 = almost always

Then tally your score.

Customer Service	
1. We check what our customers expect of us	1 2 3 4 5
2. We involve our customers in our product and service development	1 2 3 4 5
3. We know what needs our products and services meet	1 2 3 4 5
4. We listen to our customers	1 2 3 4 5
5. We respect our customers	1 2 3 4 5
6. We record and track our customer complaints	1 2 3 4 5
7. We feed our customer complaints into the product development, marketing, sales and delivery cycle	1 2 3 4 5
8. We ensure that our service to customers matches our branding and values	1 2 3 4 5
9. We work to increase the significance of our products and services to our customers	1 2 3 4 5
10. Our customers are advocates of our products and services	1 2 3 4 5
11. We allow our customers to 'try before they buy'	1 2 3 4 5
12. We know what we have promised our customers	1 2 3 4 5
13. We deliver on our promises to our customers	1 2 3 4 5
14. We have 'customer-made' products and services	1 2 3 4 5
Overall score	

How did you do?

If you scored:

28–41: You may be finding that your customers are not responding to some of your products and services. Take note of the areas where you scored the lowest, and decide upon some action today to improve your customers' experience.

56–70: You are actively building trust with your customers and should be seeing the benefits of that. Well done.

42–55: You are heading in the right direction in building trust with your customers, but you may want to work on the few areas where you had a low score.

28–41: You may be finding that your customers are not responding to some of your products and services. Take note of the areas where you scored the lowest, and decide upon some action today to improve your customers' experience.

14–27: You may be struggling to understand why you have disgruntled customers and/or high customer turnover. Now you know. Commit to a plan to help you build trust to improve your customer retention and results.

Download your FREE gift to help you build trust in your customer service. Go to www.entente.com.au/US_Book_gifts and download your FREE e-book *7 Truths about Trust Every Customer Service Person Needs to Know*. Check out the many resources and services at www.entente.com.au that can help you build trust in your customer service.

Now let's have a look at our last section on trust in business, compliance and governance, with yours truly.

18

TRUST IN COMPLIANCE AND GOVERNANCE

Innovation and new ventures fuel the global economy but the spark comes from investment. Investment is about trust. It's about knowing that the people investors entrust with their money are running ethical, transparent, and effective businesses.
—Arthur Rock, American venture capitalist

INTRODUCING VANESSA HALL

I first entered the world of compliance in the days when nobody really knew what it was. There were no guidelines that I knew of and no courses on the subject (which, believe it or not, there are today). My interest in compliance was driven by an observation I made while working for a trustee responsible for overseeing billions of dollars managed by fund managers. That trustee really had poor processes in place through which to check what all the rules were, what all the investment restrictions were (despite the fact that they were approving millions of dollars of investments daily), and whether the fund managers themselves had appropriate processes and controls in place. I was one of the first dedicated "Compliance Officers" in Australia's financial services sector.

After managing compliance strategy and process for some of Australia's largest financial institutions, I set up my own compliance and risk consulting business at the age of thirty-one. The company grew to be a team of ten and managed projects for more than forty-five clients. I always took a practical, "people" approach to compliance, governance, and risk management, preferring to understand the business strategy and goals and then help the various businesses and their departments understand the boundaries within which they operated. I worked with people to help them design processes and systems to manage the constant barrage of legislation, guidelines, industry standards, and internal policies.

As I mentioned in the introduction to this book, I decided to work at the proactive end, helping to build trust instead, although I still remain on a number of compliance committees as an external member.

TRUST VERSUS THE LAW

Trust versus the law; now that's an interesting concept. This chapter will look at how these two interact—that is, how compliance and governance are instilled in an organization—from the perspective of trust.

Let's start from the beginning.

Law: What Is It Good For?
Although I am by no means an expert in law, it appears that law has existed in some form since the dawn of time. Laws fundamentally

- Give us guidance about what is expected of us in terms of behavior or actions
- Should give us reason for the clarity of expectations: that is, what is the purpose of the law?; what need is it serving?
- Sets out the consequences of breaking the law

Laws create some sense of order, or at least that is their intent. By creating a law and "passing it down," there is an expectation by society, and the corporate world, that those laws will be followed. In fact, the pure process of setting up a business creates implicit promises—and in some cases, explicit promises—that the relevant laws will be followed.

The biggest challenge that businesses face in relation to the law is the sheer number of relevant laws, and the complexity of them. This, coupled with operating licenses, industry standards, regulator guidelines, class orders, and policy papers, makes for one hell of a headache. And that's just the "external" requirements. Companies themselves create myriad contracts, agreements, and policies that also need to be complied with.

Within every law, every policy, every contract, there is a set of expectations and needs that various stakeholders have of your company, and your company has either deliberately or inadvertently promised those stakeholders that it will carry out those things. Scary?

Indeed it is, for you are not juggling balls, you are juggling eggs!

I was thinking about the metaphor we often use in business that leaders, directors, CEOs are juggling so many balls, it is hard for them to make sure they don't drop "the ball"—any of them.

Well, knowing what we know of trust, I'd like to change that metaphor: If you are a leader, you are juggling eggs, because for every law, every contract, every policy, someone is trusting you and your company. So, if you thought compliance was boring before, or that it was just some plot to stop you from doing business, think again.

What Is Compliance?

The *Oxford English Dictionary* defines compliance as "obedience to a request, command." I spent thirteen years in compliance roles, being seen as the "company policewoman," the "thought police," "Big Brother," you name it. (One year I was even given the "Madam Lash" award at a company Christmas party, along with a set of handcuffs and a leather whip! I used to use them thereafter at work as a joke to lighten things up when I had to go and talk to someone about an issue.)

The Australasian Compliance Institute gave out coffee mugs at a conference one year with "Comply or Die" on them. Is this what compliance is really all about?

The process of compliance is basically about

1. Knowing what you are supposed to be complying with
2. Educating relevant people in your business so they are aware of the requirements
3. Putting processes and systems in place to make sure you operate in line with the "legal ENPs"
4. Checking, with some regularity, that the processes and systems actually work (that is, you are meeting the legal ENPs)
5. Making sure that people know what to do if they think there might be a problem or a breach in meeting the legal ENPs
6. Keeping the whole thing up-to-date as external and internal legal ENPs change and the business changes

Sound simple?

What Is Governance?

According to the Organisation for Economic Co-operation and Development's "Principles of Corporate Governance" (2004): "Corporate Governance involves a set of relationships between a company's management, its board, its shareholders and other stakeholders. Corporate Governance also provides the structure through which the objectives of the company are set, and the means of attaining those objectives and monitoring performance are determined...The presence of an effective corporate governance system, within an individual company and across an economy as a whole, helps to provide a degree of confidence that is necessary for the proper functioning of a market economy."

Corporate governance, then, is about relationships: how each stakeholder plays his or her part in the operation of the organization. The key players are the shareholders, board of directors, and management, but other stakeholders affected include employees, customers, suppliers, banks, regulators, the broader community, and the environment. The foundation of every relationship, as we know, is trust.

How does each stakeholder rely on the other parties to produce the outcomes he or she wants?

If we look at the "Principles of Good Corporate Governance and Best Practice Recommendations" published by the ASX in 2003, they are basically a list of all stakeholders' expectations and needs.

1. Lay solid foundations for management and oversight.
2. Structure the board to add value.
3. Promote ethical and responsible decision making.
4. Safeguard integrity in financial reporting.
5. Make timely and balanced disclosure.
6. Respect the rights of shareholders.
7. Recognize and manage risk.
8. Encourage enhanced performance.
9. Remunerate fairly and responsibly.
10. Recognize the legitimate interests of stakeholders.

You know what was amazing? I was managing my compliance and risk consultancy at the time these recommendations came out, and a lot of companies complained about having to do something about this! What we are talking about here is good business. If leaders think they can run a business without doing these basic things, they need to take a look at Enron, HIH, Worldcom, to name a few.

It's Just Another Brick in the Wall

We all know the words from this Pink Floyd song: "All in all, it's just another brick in the wall." Every time there is another issue, another corporate collapse, it is just another brick falling out of the consumers' and the regulators' ENP wall.

A breakdown of trust—not meeting expectations, not meeting needs, and not keeping promises—creates a heightened awareness of which ENPs are important in the business community. If the issues are related to a specific industry, then that entire industry is struck with more legislation, more expectations, more guidance about what is acceptable behavior, and what will not be tolerated. As long as a business exists, it is promising that it will meet the new standards, unless it lobbies against them.

It's Not Fair!

Remember in grade school when one kid would get out of line and the teacher made everyone stay in at recess? Well, the law is kind of like that. It really isn't fair, but it's where the generalizations come in. If one operator or company can find a loophole, or behave unethically, or just plain rip people off, maybe the whole industry is rife with "bad people."

I said earlier in the book that I believe that most people want to do the right thing. I found myself helping clients build systems and processes that they did not need for themselves; they were "good corporate citizens" that just got caught up in someone else's mess—the "good" children who got kept in by the teacher.

What I also found was that most organizations had poor systems and no way of tracking just what they were promising to whom, or who expected and needed what from them.

STAYING ON TOP OF THE COMPLIANCE WALL

We all need all of our stakeholders to trust us—that's a given. How, practically, do we do that? Let's take it a step at a time and base it on the process of compliance. Then we'll look at the governance side of things.

1. Know What You Are Supposed to Be Complying With

I've put these kinds of lists and spreadsheets and systems together a number of times now, and it is no mean feat. It can be difficult to know where to start. One way to get started is the top-down approach, including

- General business laws—such as corporations law, tax law, HR laws
- State based legislation—depending on where you operate
- Industry based legislation—such as construction, financial services, health

- Industry-based standards, guidance papers, and codes of ethics—usually codified by industry associations
- Company specific licenses, codes, and policies—some accepted in order to operate, some internally created
- "Department/area" specific legislation and rules (will be either federal or state laws, but a helpful way of breaking them down into manageable chunks)—such as accounting law and practice, marketing laws, customer service/complaints handling rules
- Contracts and agreements with internal and external stakeholders—including employment contracts, supplier or distributor agreements
- Department manuals and procedure documents—such as HR manuals, business continuity plans

Are all these as important as each other? Well, that depends on what party we are talking to. From a legal perspective, department manuals and procedures may not get us into trouble, but those same documents are what our business relies on to get our products and services to the market: They are the "how to" of the promises we've made to stakeholders.

I remember being asked once to quote on a project to put processes in place to help an organization meet its requirements under the privacy legislation. The board asked me what the penalty of noncompliance was for a particular process I had suggested. The "legal" penalty was around $20,000. The "trust" penalty was far worse: the possible leaking of customers' personal information. The company chose not to bother putting the process in place.

Many companies take a risk-based approach to determining which set of rules takes priority over others. At the end of the day, there are limited resources available to work through all this. The risk-based approach basically says: "What is the likelihood of something going wrong?" and "What is the consequence of something going wrong?" Based on qualitative and quantitative responses to both questions, a risk level is applied (usually high, medium, or low), and then a time frame is allocated to address the rules, based on the risk level.

From a trust perspective, I would say that if you take that the risk-based approach, make sure that one of the consequences considered is: "Can we break someone's trust if we do not attend to this? What is the ultimate cost of that broken trust?"

2. Educate Your People

What sometimes happens is that eager compliance people become frustrated at noncompliance within a business, but the people "breaking the rules" have never been told what the rules are in the first place. I've listened to boring compliance training instructing people to tell businesses "what they have to do because it's the law." Very few people ever do things "because it's the law."

Do you slow down when you drive past a school because the law says you have to, or do you slow down because you want to make sure you can stop quickly if a child suddenly runs out in front of you?

I've generally found that if people understand the intent, the "why," not just the "what," and they play a role in working out the "how," you get a much, much better result.

3. Put the Processes and Systems in Place to Meet "Legal ENPs"

This is all about doing business better, and building trust, but it involves everyone. Many businesses make the mistake of leaving this to the compliance people: "It's their job to comply." Everyone, however, has a responsibility for making sure the company keeps its legal ENPs in the area in which it works.

Melding this process with education on the various stakeholder legal ENPs helps people become a lot more aware of how they can best deliver on the company's promises.

For example, "Misleading or deceptive conduct—Section 52 of the Trade Practices Act" (why is it that so often laws are titled in the negative?) is all about making sure that we are being open, transparent, and honest in all business dealings concerning how the company and products and services are positioned, marketed, and represented.

Anybody in marketing, sales, product development, customer service, and relationship management should be educated about misleading and deceptive conduct, what it means, and the consequences. They should also be the ones responsible for the development of processes and systems to meet the requirements.

Rather than just positioning the whole thing as "This is the law, so you better comply!" looking at the whole thing from the ENPs point of view can make it more engaging. In this legal example, we are talking about what promises are being made in relation to things like

- The quality, value, or style of a product or service
- Whether the product or service is new
- Who has endorsed the product or service
- How the product or service operates and is repaired or replaced
- How much the product or service costs

The processes and systems could include two levels of checking: One division creates the product specifications and market positioning, and another division checks it before it is released to the market. Often it is the compliance person who does the second-level checking, but I don't believe it needs to be.

Although there are so many different legal ENPs sitting in so many different pieces of legislation and contracts, the processes and systems to make sure they are met are usually not complicated, and, if done well, contribute to the value of a business and it's sustainability.

4. Check That the Processes and Systems Work

We all hate the concept of an "audit." In my compliance days we used to do "monitoring," which was the same thing, really. In fact, as I would approach people to let them know we would be conducting some monitoring in their area, a common response was, "Don't you trust us?"

Trust does not mean set and forget. Guy Underwood, CEO from RISQ Group, a fraud and security risk management company, said to me during my interview with him in August 2005: "It is human nature to trust, but it can often be misplaced. It can be seen as a control against fraud and unethical behavior, but it's not an effective control. I have heard so many times, 'We had weekend barbecues together, the kids go to school together, I can't believe he would do that!' It's a betrayal of trust and it happens everywhere."

The purpose of a review is to make sure that we go back over the rules and boundaries and check that the processes and systems that are in place are still working. We also need to check that any new people understand why they do what they do, and why they need to do it a particular way.

What you find so often in business is that genuine mistakes happen. Obviously, as Guy has seen, some not-so-genuine things happen too, and that will come down to the manager understanding that particular individual's needs. (Often, something is going on personally that will drive someone to commit fraud.)

Genuine mistakes happen when

- Someone new comes into an area without induction training and/ or a lack of understanding of what happens for what reasons
- A "process improvement project" comes through to streamline processes, without considering whether there is a "legal ENPs" reason for doing things
- Someone is just not paying attention
- Someone decides to shortcut the system

The whole idea behind monitoring, checking, and audits is to make sure that all is still in order, and if it is not, to be able to highlight that so it can quickly be fixed. It is often seen as a negative process, though, and this is because too often, junior auditing people are left to conduct the review, and they work from a basic checklist. In fact, I've had a number of them in the past admit that they didn't know what they are looking for!

Another reason for the negative perception is that some overeager compliance or audit people actually get a kick out of finding something wrong. And yet another reason is that management does not position the whole monitoring process in a positive light.

When all is said and done, if you are doing something that could inadvertently break your stakeholders' trust, wouldn't you want to know so that you could fix the cracks in the wall?

5. Make Sure That People Know What to Do If They Think There Might Be a Problem

Breach reporting, whistle blowing—again, such bad stigmas are attached to them. It's looking at compliance in a negative instead of a positive, preventative light. I have seen some terrible practices in my time, and I have been pressured by senior executives to "turn a blind eye." I've even been threatened when I suggested that I thought a matter was serious and the board needed to know. And I'm not alone. In the time I ran a compliance recruitment business as part of my consultancy, I would have to say that more than 70 percent of compliance people wanted to move on because of "unethical behavior," usually around issues that nobody wanted to report or deal with.

Everyone knows that businesses are not perfect. Things go wrong from time to time—that's reality. Trying to pretend to be perfect, being proud of the fact that there is absolutely nothing on the issues and breaches register is just plain stupid, and nobody believes it anyway.

Fess up. Encourage staff to put their hand up if they think there is a problem. That good old saying "A stitch in time saves nine" is so true. If a crack starts to appear in the wall, then it is reasonable to expect that someone's trust is now being compromised.

There needs to be a good, quick, and easy reporting system that everyone knows about. Similarly, there needs to be a strong sense of "I'm doing the right thing by saying something." It can be an electronic system that sends a message up the line to management, and a dual message to your compliance manager, or even a simple sheet that is filled out.

The key is to capture the issue and have it analyzed and addressed before it gets worse. Whatever reporting system you have, it is necessary to make sure that everyone knows about it. (This connects to point 2, earlier, about educating your people.)

6. Keep It Up to Date

Things change. Businesses change. Personnel in different areas of the business change. New contracts and agreements are formed, and legislation changes. ENPs change.

Whatever processes and systems are in place need to go through a regular review. For a lot of businesses this is seen as an unnecessary, costly exercise. How often it is done, and how thoroughly, comes down to the risk: What are the consequences of having out-of-date processes and systems, or people who do not know the legal ENPs? What are the penalties? What could happen to stakeholder trust?

STAYING ON TOP OF THE GOVERNANCE WALL

OK, we've looked at staying on top of the wall from the compliance, legal rules side of things. Let's take a closer look at good corporate governance, again using the ASX's ten principles and best practice recommendations mentioned earlier. These particular principles have been designed for listed companies, but the concepts can apply to any company. To clarify one point: the principles can be found on the ASX Web site and go into great detail about what is expected of listed companies. I am not trying to replicate that. I am merely using the headings as a guide, and looking at the subject from a trust perspective.

In addition, this section is directed to leaders of organizations, so when I say "you," I am speaking to directors, CEOs, business owners, and executive managers.

The principles themselves appear to be very commonsensical, like they are telling you how to boil an egg. What they are really saying is how to protect eggs!

1. Lay Solid Foundations for Management and Oversight

This principle is about clarifying roles and responsibilities of the board and management. If you are a one-man band, this concept still applies to the extent that you need to clarify for yourself what it is that you actually do—your strategy. I've found that small operators usually perform better with some form of mentoring, coaching, or advisory input, in which case, you need to clarify those roles.

For those in larger organizations, this is about managing expectations, clarifying needs, and articulating promises of what others will get as a result of the board and management performing their role, and what you get as a result. This is about accountability. It's also about honesty. Leaders should not commit to some one, to their company, or to their board what they cannot deliver. If you have doubts, express them. Determine what support you need in order to carry out your function. This is about building trust.

2. Structure the Board to Add Value

Gone are the days of the quick board meeting so directors can get in a good round of golf in the afternoon. The board, or any kind of management committee, is representing shareholders (even if that shareholder is just you). There needs to be a blend of skills and personalities on the board.

I am the sole director of Entente, but I have a management committee, and they sometimes give me a hard time. Why? Because they question me. They challenge me. They make me think: "OK, so that sounded like a good idea, but is it the right thing for the business right now? Can we afford to do it now, or should it wait?" They are there to protect me as a major shareholder, and my business is stronger for it.

You don't want yes-men agreeing with everything you do, while cracks are appearing in the wall and elsewhere bricks are falling out. What you want are "engineers," people who will say: "You know, if you do that, you'll lose a few bricks out of the expectations and needs walls, and you'll drop a couple of those explicit promises. Are you prepared to clean up the mess?"

3. Promote Ethical and Responsible Decision Making

How should leaders behave in your organization? If you have people in a position to affect and influence the strategy and operation of the business and its sustainability, don't you want to know on what basis they make decisions? Your organization's values should clearly state what is acceptable and what you expect from your people, but they should also be a statement about how the directors and leadership team will behave.

The overall needs of the company should be considered: What is it we are trying to achieve, and what decisions could influence that? Who has the power to make those decisions, and do they understand the responsibility they hold? Are they "trustworthy"?

4. Safeguard Integrity in Financial Reporting

If there is one area in business that seems to consistently come under question, it is whether the financials of the company are accurately represented. Why is this the case? Because there is often a conflict between stakeholder expectations and needs and what is financially viable in business. There is constant pressure on business to pay employees more, provide more benefits, provide better returns, and reduce prices on products and services. Seriously, if everyone got what they expected, a business could easily go out of business!

Financial reporting provides great indicators of business viability and sustainability, if it is accurate. It may not tell you what you want to know, but if it is done properly, it tells you exactly what you need to know.

Taking this seriously, as most companies do, is vital to your ability to know what promises you can comfortably make. Having an independent audit on your financials (as many company structures are required to do) should be a good safeguard to the integrity of the reporting; however, the best people to know whether the information is accurate are those who are close to the action. Getting management involved in understanding and checking financials for their business area creates accountability for performance. Being open and transparent about what is really going on is paramount to keeping trust intact.

5. Make Timely and Balanced Disclosures

To disclose is to reveal, to make known. This is openness and transparency, but it is even more detailed than that. This is about when to make something known, and doing that in a balanced way; that is, presenting both the "good" news and the "bad."

Being open about something months after the event is not being transparent, and it's not acting with integrity. It might alleviate some guilt for yourself and make it "appear" that you were doing the right thing, but it may not benefit others involved.

Disclosure from a business perspective, and from a listed company perspective, is about letting investors know about things going on with the business: This includes the financial situation, how the company is performing, and how it is being managed. It is about letting investors know when anything changes that might have an impact on their decision to continue to invest.

Disclosure is about managing expectations, and giving people timely information so they can assess whether the company is able to meet their needs.

6. Respect the Rights of Shareholders

Shareholders are the owners of the company. They have invested a certain amount of money in good faith that the promises made by the leaders of that company will be kept. They have expectations and needs.

Although charities and other company structures may be different, there are still others who are providing funds to enable that company, business, or organization to function. They, too, have expectations and needs.

Recognition of this, communicating with shareholders, giving them information, and allowing them to participate in meetings (general meetings for listed companies) gives them a chance to see that you are keeping the wall intact and protecting their trust.

7. Recognize Risk and Manage It

I talked earlier about risk, but it is something that a lot of businesses don't focus on. Often, when we do go through the process of identifying risks, we find out things we wish we didn't know! Having said that, trust cannot be built while your head is buried in the sand. Remember that courage and decisiveness are two of the qualities of a trustworthy person, and it takes leaders with these qualities to really identify, assess, manage, and monitor risks in business.

The process of identifying risks often starts with a SWOT analysis, which looks at your strengths, weaknesses, opportunities, and threats. While many people start off by only looking at the weaknesses and threats, you also risk losing your strengths and missing opportunities. Your biggest risk in business is breaking down the trust of any of your stakeholders.

Getting your people involved in all the stages of risk management is important. They will have insights into what could go wrong, for example, or what process you need in order to identify opportunities you don't have. The processes and systems that you then build throughout your business to manage the various risks will help you identify any cracks in your wall.

8. Encourage Enhanced Performance

This is all about accountability. How do the stakeholders know if the board and management have performed? What should the outcome be? How is it measured? What happens if that outcome is not achieved?

One of the things that people within the business look for is accountability in the leaders. The need for fairness, equity, and respect of others all hang on the consequences of good or poor performance. Shareholders are obviously looking to see that the operation of the business is being taken seriously and that the board, committees, individual directors, and key executives are being assessed.

This has a direct link to the ability of shareholders and employees to trust in the leadership of the business. Unfortunately, it is one area in which many businesses fail abysmally. Why? Often individual needs are allowed to outweigh the needs of the business. Massive conflicts of interests arise and are dealt with badly. Each time this happens there is a sacrifice: one egg temporarily saved and dozens, hundreds, thousands of others broken. I say temporarily because, for example, while allowing someone to perform badly and still keep his or her job may satisfy that employee's immediate need for money, it will break down needs for respect, self-confidence, and morality. It will also create a sense of confusion around expectations (such as, Is the person accountable or not?). Cracks will still appear in the employee's wall, and in fact, it will most likely break at some point.

9. Remunerate Fairly and Responsibly

Stakeholders have an expectation of fair remuneration and a need for fairness and equity in how they and others are treated. This is one area that has come under scrutiny in recent times for good reason. The "ASX Guidelines" actually state, "It is important that there be a clear relationship between performance and remuneration, and that the policy underlying executive remuneration be understood by investors."

When there is little to no communication about why there is such discrepancy between executive remuneration and employee remuneration, it creates confusion among stakeholders. From confusion come gossip, anger, a lack of respect, and a sense of injustice. You cannot achieve enhanced performance when you have a bunch of angry people working for you.

If there is justification for the level of remuneration that is linked to performance, then communicate this to stakeholders. Create understanding; from it come tolerance, respect, and a sense of fairness. If there is no justification for the level of remuneration, especially if there has been poor performance, just don't go there—it is a recipe for disaster. Someone will be treading on a lot of eggshells!

10. Recognize the Legitimate Interests of Stakeholders

By "legitimate interests," the ASX guidelines are talking about "legal and other obligations" to stakeholders, including employees, clients/customers, and the broader community. This is about managing the ENPs of all your stakeholders.

Who are all your stakeholders? What do they expect of you as a business? What do they need from you? What have you promised them?

Having clear guidelines and processes in place that identify and address these critical questions is the key to building and maintaining trust in business. What more can I say?

STAKEHOLDER ENPS

I covered in simple terms just what compliance and governance are really all about, as well as the role trust plays in that. There are some basic things that you should be doing to build trust with your stakeholders, including shareholders and regulators. I've created some questions here for you to contemplate.

Do this quick assessment and check your score at the end. Rate each question on the scale of 1 to 5:

1 = almost never

2 = rarely

3 = sometimes

4 = frequently

5 = almost always

Then tally your score.

Compliance and Governance	
1. We have systems and processes to track what we are supposed to be complying with	1 2 3 4 5
2. We include ENPs® from contracts and Service Level Agreements in our review process	1 2 3 4 5
3. We conduct regular training so people know what they are supposed to be complying with	1 2 3 4 5
4. We make sure our systems and processes facilitate easy compliance	1 2 3 4 5
5. We make sure our process improvement projects first check Legal ENPs®	1 2 3 4 5
6. We have a reporting process for issues and breaches	1 2 3 4 5
7. We protect people who report issues and breaches	1 2 3 4 5
8. We follow a process that assesses new laws to update systems and processes where needed	1 2 3 4 5
9. We follow a process that assesses new contracts and policies to update systems and processes where needed	1 2 3 4 5
10. We are timely in our open and transparent disclosure to stakeholders	1 2 3 4 5
11. We manage our business risks	1 2 3 4 5
12. We remunerate executives fairly	1 2 3 4 5
Overall score	

How did you do?

If you scored:

- 48–60: You are doing well in building trust in your compliance and governance. Well done.
- 36–47: You are well on the way to building trust. Make a note of the areas you need to work on and get to it.

24–35: You have some work to do and may be feeling the effects of a breakdown of stakeholder trust. Take note of the areas where your scores were low and put an action plan in place—today!

12–23: You may well be having some problems in the business and are probably spending money fixing mistakes that shouldn't have happened. You may want to get some advice and support as to the best way to build trust back into your business and improve your results.

Download your FREE gift to help you build trust in your compliance and governance. Go to www.entente.com.au/US_Book_gifts and download your FREE e-book *7 Truths about Trust Every Risk Manager Needs to Know*. Check out the many resources and services at www.entente.com.au that can help you build trust in your compliance and governance.

CONCLUSION

I did want to just wrap up the book by saying thank you once again to the people who contributed their thoughts to help readers gain greater insight into building trust in business.

My son, Lachlan, has been reading sections of this book over my shoulder, and he is still amazed that much of this has come from him bringing home that Mother's Day present I shared at the beginning of the book. I am grateful for his honesty and wisdom.

I hope that you have learned from this book and that it helps you achieve even greater success in your business life.

Please check out www.thetruthabouttrust.com and www.entente.com.au for more tools and tips to help you build trust in business. You can also order copies of our small book "The Simple Truth About Trust," a perfect summary of the Trust Model for your employees, friends, and family.

Entente has created a library of trust-related articles, papers, books, and other references for you to consult as you find out more about trust. We have sorted them into the six categories we have covered in this book. This library grows on an almost daily basis, and you can help us continue to ensure its value by sending us links to relevant and helpful resources as you find them. E-mail info@entente.com.au.

If you would like me to come and speak at your conference or other events, or you would like me to advise your business on how to improve on building trust, I can be booked through www.entente.com.au.

For help in measuring trust in your business, for workshops, or pro-grams from accredited consultants, visit www.entente.com.au.

Thank you for coming on this journey through trust with me.